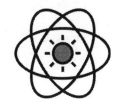

SAT PHYSICS

5 Full Practice Test

for Physics Subject Test

2017 edition

In Remembrance of

King Bhumibol Adulyadej

About Author:

Ankur Sharma is an experienced professor who had been teaching math and physics for more than fifteen years at AIMS located in Thailand. He earned a B.Engineering a M.SC in TechnologyManagement from Assumption College with full scholarship. Most of the students who studied SAT Physics and Math had pass the exam easily with a score of 650 above

His goal for writing this book was to help students and examinee to use the time efficiently thru the right material with a proper method.

For more inquiries please email: ker999@gmail.com

ISBN-13: 978-1541350434

ISBN-10: 154135043X

BISAC: Education / Adult & Continuing Education

CONTENTS

Topics on exam

Mechanics (about 36% to 42%)

- **Kinematics**, such as velocity, acceleration, motion in one dimension, and motion of projectiles
- **Dynamics**, such as force, Newton's laws, statics, and friction
- **Energy and momentum**, such as potential and kinetic energy, work, power, impulse, and conservation laws
- **Circular motion**, such as uniform circular motion and centripetal force
- **Simple harmonic motion**, such as mass on a spring and the pendulum
- **Gravity**, such as the law of gravitation, orbits, and Kepler's laws

Electricity and magnetism (about 18% to 24%)

- **Electric fields, forces, and potentials**, such as Coulomb's law, induced charge, field and potential of groups of point charges, and charged particles in electric fields
- **Capacitance**, such as parallel-plate capacitors and time-varying behavior in charging/ discharging
- **Circuit elements and DC circuits**, such as resistors, light bulbs, series and parallel networks, Ohm's law, and Joule's law
- **Magnetism**, such as permanent magnets, fields caused by currents, particles in magnetic fields, Faraday's law, and Lenz's law

Waves and optics (about 15% to 19%)

- **General wave properties**, such as wave speed, frequency, wavelength, superposition, standing wave diffraction, and Doppler effect
- **Reflection and refraction**, such as Snell's law and changes in wavelength and speed
- **Ray optics**, such as image formation using pinholes, mirrors, and lenses
- **Physical optics**, such as single-slit diffraction, double-slit interference, polarization, and color

Heat and thermodynamics (about 6% to 11%)

- **Thermal properties**, such as temperature, heat transfer, specific and latent heats, and thermal expansions
- **Laws of thermodynamics**, such as first and second laws, internal energy, entropy, and heat engine efficiency

Modern physics (about 6% to 11%)

- **Quantum phenomena**, such as photons and photoelectric effect
- **Atomic**, such as the Rutherford and Bohr models, atomic energy levels, and atomic spectra
- **Nuclear and particle physics**, such as radioactivity, nuclear reactions, and fundamental particles
- **Relativity**, such as time dilation, length contraction, and mass-energy equivalence

Miscellaneous (about 4% to 9%)

- **General**, such as history of physics and general questions that overlap several major topics
- **Analytical skills**, such as graphical analysis, measurement, and math skills
- **Contemporary physics**, such as astrophysics, superconductivity, and chaos theory

credit:

https://collegereadiness.collegeboard.org/sat-subject-tests/subjects/science/physics

What's inside SAT Physics subject test ?

SAT Physics subject test requires you to have at least one year of introduction to pre-college physics and basic knowledge of algebra and trigonometry. It is also advisable that you have some experience in the laboratory experiment.

You will be tested upon fundamental concepts and knowledge, single-concept problem, and mixed concept problem.

Remember that all the formulas require you to convert everything to SI-base units before using them to obtain a correct result.

How to calculate the score ?

Raw score = number of correct answers - (0.25 x number of wrong answers)

The raw score is then converted using a curved calculation for overall score into range of 200 to 800.

Tips and Tricks

About the test:

    i.   No calculator is allowed

    ii.   There are 75 questions multiple choice

    iii.   60 minutes is the time limit

    iv.   1 correct gives 1 point

    v.   1 wrong gets minus 1/4 point

    vi.   A blank gives 0 point

    vii.   Total full score is 800

Guide-line in taking the test:

    i.   Time yourself

    ii.   Do easy question first

    iii.   Each question is awarded same mark

    iv.   Pace yourself after 5-6 questions

    v.   Round the numbers for easy calculation

    vi.   Double check your work for units

    vii.   Write the formula out

    viii.   Draw out the diagram for visualization

    ix.   Eliminate choices

    x.   Be confident in yourself

How to use this book ?

Guide-line in using this book :

1. *Time is key number one*

This book has a timer that help you pace yourself by looking at the <u>top-right corner</u> you will notice a sand watch

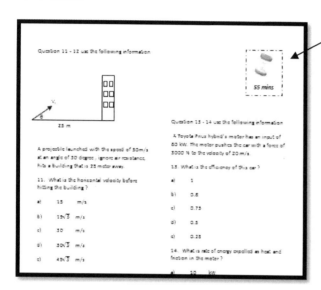

2. *Draw the diagram and list the formula out*

The key here is to <u>draw</u> out or <u>list what we know</u> to see a picture of how to solve the problem

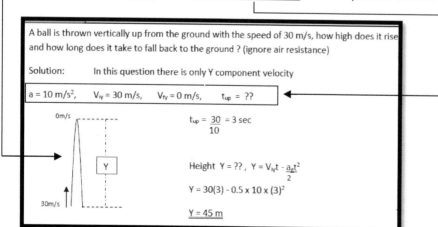

3. *Rounding numbers in calculation makes life easy*

Round the numbers for easy calculation using some tricks below

7. Marry-go-round has a radius of 35 m took about 10 second to complete one revolution. What is its angular velocity ?

a) 0.14 rad/s
b) 0.24 rad/s
c) 0.53 rad/s
d) 0.63 rad/s
e) 0.77 rad/s

$\omega = \Delta\theta/\Delta t = 2\pi/10 = (2 \times 3.14) / 10$

$= 6.28/10 = 0.628 = 0.63$ rad/s

move the decimal point forward once and round up

4. *Eliminate choices and make an educated guess*

Which of the following method is used to find the lower fixed point in a thermometer ?

a) put thermometer in boiling water

b) put thermometer in melting ice

c) put thermometer in boiling mercury

d) put thermometer in melting mercury

e) put thermometer in boiling alcohol

we should cut 'c' , 'd' and 'e' out first since mercury and alcohol are used in thermometer

Lower means **ice melts**, so cut 'a' out

Pre-Test

Difficulty level

★★★★★

60 mins

Question 1 - 5 use the following information

a) Newton's law of inertia

b) Newton's second law of motion

c) Newton's third law of motion

d) Newton's law of gravitational

e) Kepler's law of planetary motion

Match the concept to the following law:

1. All planets orbit the Sun

2. A paper is pulled out from a text book without the text book moving or sliding

3. Throwing a baseball directly into the wall causing it to bounce back

4. The moon orbits the Earth in circular path

5. Pushing a man on a wheel-chair requires more force than pushing an empty chair

Question 6 - 10 use the following information

a) A·s

b) $kg \cdot m \, s^{-2}$

c) $kg \, m^{-1} \, s^{-2}$

d) V·A

e) W·s

Match the following unit to the quantity:

6. Power

7. Charge

8. Force

9. Pressure

10. Energy

Question 11 - 12 use the following information

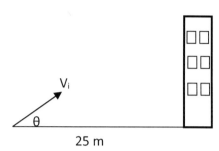

25 m

A projectile launched with the speed of 30m/s at an angle of 30 degree , ignore air resistance, hits a building that is 25 meter away.

11. What is the horizontal velocity before hitting the building ?

a)   15   m/s

b) $15\sqrt{3}$ m/s

c)   30   m/s

d) $30\sqrt{3}$ m/s

e) $45\sqrt{3}$ m/s

12. How long does the projectile takes to reach the building ?

a)   0.45   s

b)   0.75   s

c)   0.96   s

d)   1.23   s

e)   1.64   s

Question 13 - 14 use the following information

A Toyota Prius hybrid's motor has an input of 80 kW. The motor pushes the car with a force of 3000 N to the velocity of 20 m/s.

13. What is the efficiency of this car ?

a)   1

b)   0.8

c)   0.75

d)   0.5

e)   0.25

14. What is rate of energy expelled as heat and friction in the motor ?

a)   10   kW

b)   20   kW

c)   40   kW

d)   120   kW

e)   140   kW

SAT Physics Practice-Test

50 mins

15. The current in the river flows at the rate of 5 m/s. If a boat is to move 3 km thru river in 2 minutes at what speed should it move and in which direction ?

a)   155 m/s with current

b)   155 m/s against current

c)   20 m/s against current

d)   20 m/s with the current

e)   25 m/s with the current

16. If the distance between the Earth and the Moon is tripled, what is the effect on the gravitational force between them ?

a)   increased by 3 times

b)   increased by 9 times

c)   remain the same

d)   decreased by 1/3

e)   decreased by 1/9

17. Which of the following is NOT TRUE about Kepler's law of planetary motion ?

a)   All planets orbit the Sun

b)   A planet's move faster when it's close to the Sun

c)   All planets have an elliptical orbital path

d)   A planet's move slower when it's further from the Sun

e)   Kepler's constant is calculated by the ratio mean radius cube to period square root

18. The new Porsche claims that is engine can do zero to 30 m/s in 3 seconds. How much distance is moved during this 3 seconds ?

a)   15   m

b)   30   m

c)   35   m

d)   40   m

e)   45   m

19. Which of the following is true about the time taken by the satellite to orbits the Earth?

a) same time as Moon orbits the Earth

b) same time as Earth rotates around itself

c) same time as Earth orbits the Sun

d) same time as Moon rotates around itself

e) same time as Earth orbits around the Moon

20. Which of the following value(s) remain constant throughout the flight ?

	Horizontal component	Vertical component
a)	Velocity	Velocity
b)	Acceleration	Velocity
c)	Velocity	Acceleration
d)	Acceleration	Acceleration
e)	Displacement	Velocity

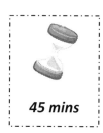

Question 21 - 23 use the following information

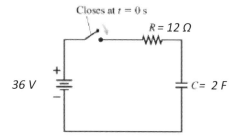

21. How much current will flow thru the resistor at the instant switch is closed ?

a)   0   A

b)   1   A

c)   1.5   A

d)   2   A

e)   3   A

22. How much charge is stored in a capacitor after a while ?

a)   2   C

b)   9   C

c)   18   C

d)   38   C

e)   72   C

23. What is the current in the circuit after the capacitor is fully charged and the switch is still closed ?

a)   0   A

b)   1   A

c)   1.5   A

d)   2   A

e)   3   A

SAT Physics Practice-Test

24. A piston has a volume of 12 cm^3 compressed the gas at atmospheric pressure to the volume of 8 cm^3, how much work was done ?

a)   0.404   J

b)   4.04   J

c)   40.4   J

d)   404   J

e)   4040   J

Question 25 - 27 use the following information

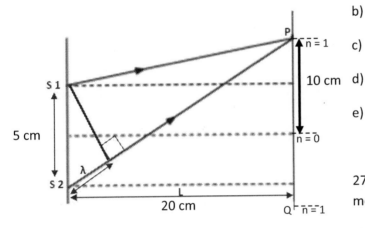

A monochromatic light passes through the double slit

25. What is the value of the wavelength (λ) of this light ?

a)   2   cm

b)   2.5   cm

c)   4   cm

d)   4.5   cm

e)   5   cm

26. If we double the distance between the slits, what is the value of the distance between the fringes ?

a)   2.5   cm

b)   5   cm

c)   10   cm

d)   15   cm

e)   20   cm

27. Which of the following is true about the monochromatic light wave ?

a)   All waves have same wavelength

b)   All waves travel at the same frequency

c)   All waves have same phase

d)   All wave have same amplitude

e)   Light wave that display only one color

28. Two waves are producing a beat of 5 Hz, which of the following could be the frequency of another wave if one of the wave has a frequency of 500 Hz

        (I)   495 Hz

        (II)   100 Hz

        (III)   505 Hz

a)   (I) only

b)   (II) only

c)   (I) and (II) only

d)   (I) and (III) only

e)   (II) and (III) only

29. Light strikes a mirror at perpendicularly, what is the angle of reflection ?

a)   0°

b)   30°

c)   45°

d)   60°

e)   90°

30. A tuning fork vibrates into a bottle with a frequency of 250 Hz, given that the speed of sound in air is 340 m/s. What is the length of the bottle ?

a)   25   cm

b)   34   cm

c)   250   cm

d)   340   cm

e)   590   cm

Question 31 -33 refer to the diagram

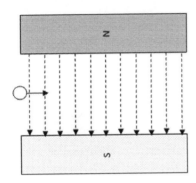

A charge of 5 Coulomb moving with a speed of 12 m/s passes thru a magnetic field of 8 Tesla.

31. If the charge is an electron, which of the following will be the direction of the force created ?

a)   into the page

b)   out of the page

c)   top of the page

d)   bottom of the page

e)   westward

32. How much force is experienced by the charge ?

a)   60   N

b)   120   N

c)   480   N

d)   610   N

e)   825   N

33. If the magnetic field and velocity of the charge is doubled, what would be the effect of force experienced by the charge ?

a)   reduced by half

b)   reduced by a quarter

c)   doubled

d)   quadrupled

e)   stay the same

34. A space-ship travels thru the galaxy for 1 year space time, when it came back on Earth the time on Earth have passed 2 years. At what speed was it travelling in space ? (Given that C is the speed of light)

a) $\frac{\sqrt{3}}{2}$ C

b) $\sqrt{3}$ C

c)   C

d) $\frac{1}{2}$ C

e) $\frac{\sqrt{5}}{2}$ C

35. Which of the following event can occur in transverse wave but not longitudinal wave ?

a)   Interference

b)   refraction

c)   reflection

d)   polarization

e)   diffraction

36. What is the total resistance of the circuit below ?

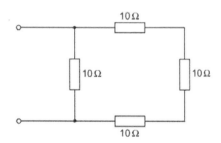

a)   4   Ω

b)   7.5   Ω

c)   20   Ω

d)   35   Ω

e)   40   Ω

37. A battery with an e.m.f. of 12 V has an internal resistance of one ohm is connected to a heater with a resistance of 5 Ω. What is the power dissipated by the heater ?

a)   12.5   W

b)   20.0   W

c)   28.8   W

d)   32.5   W

e)   60.0   W

38. Which of the following combination of resistors can give a total resistance of 5 Ω ?

	Number of 4Ω connected in parallel	Number of 4Ω connected in series
a)	2	2
b)	2	1
c)	3	1
d)	3	2
e)	4	1

39. Two negative charges of 20 C and 5 C are placed a distance of 11 meter apart. At which point from the 20 C charge would the electric field be equal to zero ?

a)   2.67   m

b)   3.67   m

c)   4.33   m

d)   6.67   m

e)   7.33   m

20 mins

Question 40 - 44 refer to the information below

a) Amplitude

b) Extension

c) Period

d) Mass

e) Elastic limit

A spring undergoes a vertical oscillation once the mass is compressed a distance of x cm, ignoring frictional loss.

40. Frequency is inversely proportional to the square root of the

41. If the spring is compressed a distance of 2x centimeter, it would cause an increase in

42. Force applied by the load is directly proportional to the

43. The ratio of wavelength to wave speed is equal to the

44. Hooke's law can be used until reached the maximum

Question 45 - 46 refer to the following information

Two kilogram of water in a beaker is heated from 20 °C to 40 °C by an electric heater of one kilowatt, given that specific heat capacity of water is 4200 J/kg°c.

45. If the heater was turned on for 5 minutes then how much heat is loss to the surrounding ?

a)   72   kJ

b)   132   kJ

c)   168   kJ

d)   300   kJ

e)   468   kJ

46. Which of the following remain constant while the heat is supplied to it ?

a)   volume

b)   temperature

c)   specific heat capacity

d)   energy of water molecules

e)   speed of water molecules

SAT Physics Practice-Test

47. A gas exerts the energy by pushing the piston from 30 cm³ mark to 35 cm³ mark if the gas inside the piston is at 1.5 atm, how much work is done by the gas ?

a)   0.34   J

b)   0.42   J

c)   0.53   J

d)   0.76   J

e)   0.93   J

48. Four hundred joules of heat are added to an isolated system, while the system does three hundred joules of work. What is the change in the internal energy of this system ?

a)   50   J

b)   100   J

c)   -50   J

d)   -100   J

e)   700   J

49. First law of thermodynamic is related to which law ?

a) law of conservation of momentum

b) law of conservation of kinetic energy

c) law of conservation of energy

d) law of conservation of molecules

e) law of conversion of mass and energy

50. A 300 N force is applied to 20 kg box horizontally, the friction between the block and the floor is 60 N. What is the acceleration of the box ?

a)   18   m/s²

b)   12   m/s²

c)   10   m/s²

d)   8   m/s²

e)   6   m/s²

51. When the speed of the object doubled which of the following must be true ?

(I)   Kinetic energy doubled

(II)   Kinetic energy quadrupled

(III)   Internal energy is increased

a)   (I) only

b)   (II) only

c)   (III) only

d)   (I) and (III) only

e)   (II) and (III) only

52. What is the tangential velocity of a disk with radius of 2 cm that spin at the rate of 30 rev/min ?

a)   2.34   cm/s

b)   6.28   cm/s

c)   12.3   cm/s

d)   23.4   cm/s

e)   60   cm/s

53. A load of 5.5 N is applied on a spring, the extension of the spring is 10 cm. How much work was done by extending the spring ?

a)   0.275   J

b)   0.55   J

c)   0.65   J

d)   0.975   J

e)   1.25   J

54. Which of the following must be TRUE about a magnetic field produced by a current carrying wire ?

a) the field is uniform

b) the field lines are circles about the wire

c) the field strength increases as the distance increases

d) the field line is parallel to the wire and directed outward

e) the field line is parallel to the wire and directed inward

55. Which device's resistance changes as temperature change ?

a)   LDR

b)   Thermistor

c)   Rheostat

d)   Potential divider

e)   Diode

56. A transformer that has an a.c. input voltage power of 500 watts is used as a step-up transformer. Which of the following is true about this transformer ?

(I) Power input = Power output

(II) Input current is larger than output current

(III) Input voltage is smaller than output voltage

a)   (I) only

b)   (II) only

c)   (III) only

d)   (I) and (III) only

e)   (II) and (III) only

Question 57 - 59 use the information below

Visible light enters the glass that has a
refractive index of 1.41

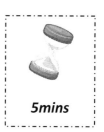

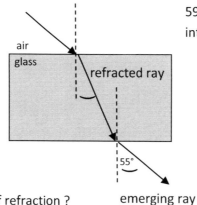

57. What is the angle of refraction ?

    a)   13.0°

    b)   24.3°

    c)   25.6°

    d)   31.3°

    e)   35.5°

58. What is the speed of light in this glass ?

    a) 1.97×10^8 m /s

    b) 2.13×10^8 m/s

    c) 2.43×10^8 m/s

    d) 3×10^8 m/s

    e) 4.23×10^8 m/s

59. At what angle of refraction will the total
internal reflection take place ?

    a)   33.0°

    b)   41.3°

    c)   45.2°

    d)   53.3°

    e)   61.1°

60. If an electromagnetic wave of frequency
greater than threshold frequency falls on a
metal plate, which of the following particle will
be given off ?

    a)   photon

    b)   proton

    c)   photoelectron

    d)   neutron

    e)   anti-neutrino

Answer Key (Pre-Test)

Question	Answer	Explanation
1.	E	According to Kepler's law of planetary motion, all planets orbits the Sun in an elliptical path
2.	A	This illustrates law of inertia or first law of motion
3.	C	Action force = Reaction force This is Newton's third law of motion
4.	D	Two bodies in space will attract each other, this is Newton's law of gravitational
5.	B	According to second law (F = ma) Mass is directly proportional to force applied
6.	D	Power = V x I (Volt) (Ampere)
7.	A	Charge = I x T (Ampere) (Second)
8.	B	Force = m x a (kilogram) (m/s^2)
9.	C	Pressure = Force / Area (kg m/s^2) / (m^2)
10.	E	Energy = Power x time (watts) x (second)
11.	B	$V_x = V_i \cos \theta = 30 \cos(30) = 15\sqrt{3}$ m/s
12.	C	V_x = distance / time Time = distance/ V_x Time = $25 / 15\sqrt{3}$ = 0.96 second
13.	C	P_{out} / P_{in} = (F x V) / (80 k) = (3000 x 20) / (80 k) = 6/8 = 0.75
14.	B	Power loss = P_{in} - P_{out} = 80k - 60k = 20 kW
15.	D	We need to calculated the speed first Speed = distance / time = 3000 m / 120 second Speed = 25 m/s Speed that boat should move = 25 - 5 = 20 m/s with the current (help)
16.	E	Force is inversely proportional to radius square F_1 x R_1^2 = F_2 x R_2^2 F_1 (R)^2 = F_2 (R/3)^2 F_2 = F_1 / 9 Reduced by 1/9

Question	Answer	Explanation
17.	E	The ratio of Kepler's constant is the ratio mean radius cube to period square
18.	E	u = 0 m/s, t = 3 sec, v = 30m/s, s = ?? s = (v + u) t/2 s = (0 + 30) 3/2 = 45 meters
19.	B	The only correct choice here is (B) in order to escape from the Earth's gravitational pull we must move at the same orbital speed of the Earth
20.	C	Horizontal velocity always remain the same and acceleration of vertical component is due to gravity which will also remain the same
21.	E	V = I R 36 = I (12) I = 3 A
22.	E	Q = C V Q = 2 x 36 Q = 72 Couloumb
23.	A	Once the capacitor is fully charged and the switch is still closed, it will not discharged any charge out. Therefore the current in the circuit will be zero
24.	A	Atmospheric pressure = 1 atm or 101 kPa Work = P x ΔV Work = 101 k x (4 x 10^{-6}) Work = 0.404 J
25.	B	$\dfrac{\lambda}{D} = \dfrac{x}{L}$ $\dfrac{\lambda}{5} = \dfrac{10}{20}$ λ = 2.5 cm
26.	B	If we double the distance between the slits (D) then distance between the fringes will **decrease by half** (x), because D is inversely proportional to x $\dfrac{\lambda}{D} = \dfrac{x}{L}$ $\dfrac{2.5}{10} = \dfrac{x}{20}$ x = 5 cm
27.	D	All of the following are the properties of monochromatic except D

Question	Answer	Explanation
28.	D	Difference between the two frequency must be 5 Hz $\| 500 - f \| = 5$ Hz
29.	A	Perpendicularly striking means angle of incidence is zero, therefore angle of reflection will be zero as well
30.	B	$v = f \times \lambda$ $340 = 250 \times \lambda$ $\lambda = 1.36$ m Since its one closed end we use $L = \lambda / 4$ $L = 1.36/4$ $L = 0.34$ m or 34 cm
31.	B	According to Flemings Rule we can apply the right hand (3-D) rule here We will obtain the force pointing out of the page
32.	C	$F = q v B$ $F = 5 \times 12 \times 8 = 480$ N
33.	D	$F = q v B$ If we doubled B and v then F will be 4 times greater or quadrupled for 'q' to remain the same
34.	A	$$T = \frac{t_0}{\sqrt{1 - (v/c)^2}}$$ We know that T = 2 and t_0 = 1 year Plugging in and rearrange the formula we will obtain $1 - (v/c)^2 = 1/4$ $(v/c)^2 = 3/4$ $v = \frac{\sqrt{3}}{2} C$
35.	D	Transverse wave can be interfere, refract, reflect , diffract and polarized Longitunal wave have already been polarized, so it cannot be polarized further

Question	Answer	Explanation
36.	B	 $1 / R_{total} = 1/10 + 1/30$ $R_{total} = 7.5\ \Omega$
37.	B	V = e.m.f. - Ir IR = e.m.f. - Ir $I = e.m.f. / (r + R)$ $I = 12 / (1 + 5)$ $I = 2\ A$ Power dissipated $= I^2 R$ Power dissipated $= (2)^2 \times 5 = 20\ W$
38.	E	Four 4Ω in parallel $1/R = 1/4 + 1/4 + 1/4 + 1/4$ $R = 1\ \Omega$ Four 4Ω in parallel and 1 series $R_{total} = 1 + 4 = 5\ \Omega$
39.	E	Electric field on both charges should be equal to cancle out $E_1 = E_2$ $(E = kq/r^2)$ $k(-20)/x^2 = k(-5)/(11-x)^2$ $4(11-x)^2 = x^2$ $2(11-x) = x$ $x = 22/3$ meter or 7.33 meter from 20 C
40.	D	$f = \dfrac{\sqrt{k}}{2\pi\sqrt{m}}$ frequency is inversely proportional to square root of mass
41.	A	If the spring is compressed a distance of 2x centimeter, it would cause an increase in energy or amplitude of oscillation is greater

Question	Answer	Explanation
42.	B	$F = k X$ Force applied by the load is directly proportional to the 'extension'
43.	C	$V = f \lambda$ $V = \lambda / t$ $t = \lambda / V$ t is the period
44.	E	Hooke's law can be used until reached the maximum ' Elastic limit' is reached
45.	B	Energy loss = energy supply - energy required to heat water from 20 to 40°C Energy loss = P x t - m c Δt = 1000 x 300 - 2 x 4200 x 20 = 132000 Joules
46.	C	Specific heat capacity of a substance doesn't change at all
47.	D	Pressure = 1.5 atm = 1.5 x 101 kPa = 151.5 k $\Delta V = 35 - 30 = 5$ cm^3 Work = P x ΔV Work = 151.5 x 10^3 x (5 x 10^{-6}) Work = 0.76 J
48.	B	$Q = \Delta U + W$ $400 = \Delta U + 300$ $\Delta U = 100$ Joules
49.	C	First law of thermodynamic is analogous to law of conservation of energy $Q = \Delta U + W$
50.	B	$F_{net} = F - f$ $F_{net} = 300 - 60$ ma = 240 N a = 12 m/s^2
51.	E	$KE = 1/2 m v^2$ If V is doubled then KE is quadrupled , this lead to increase in internal energy also
52.	B	$\omega = 2 \pi f = 2 \pi (30/60) = \pi$ $V = \omega R = \pi$ x 2 = 6.28 cm/s
53.	A	Work = 1/2 F x X = 1/2 x 5.5 x 0.1 = 0.275 J

Question	Answer	Explanation
54.	B	According to right hand grip rule the field line will move in circular shape around a current carrying wire
55.	B	Thermistor's resistance varies inversely as temperature
56.	D	In a transformer → total input power = total output power The transformer is step-up, which means voltage is increased on the output side
57.	E	Air Glass $n_1 \sin\theta_1 \quad = \quad n_2 \sin\theta_2$ $1(\sin 55) = \quad 1.41 \sin(r)$ $r \quad\quad = \quad 35.5°$
58.	B	Air Glass $n_1 V_1 \quad = \quad n_2 V_2$ $1(3 \times 10^8) = \quad 1.41\, V_2$ $V_2 \quad = \quad 2.13 \times 10^8$ m/s
59.	C	$n \quad = \quad 1 / \sin C$ $1.41 = \quad 1 / \sin C$ $C \quad = \quad 45.2°$
60.	C	This is known as photo-electric effect on a metal therefore a 'photo-electron' will be given off

Score Range

Raw Score	Conversion
58 - 60	800
54 - 57	750 - 790
50 - 53	720 - 740
45 - 49	690 - 710
40 - 44	650 - 680
35 - 39	590 - 640
30 - 34	540 - 580
25 - 29	510 - 530
20 - 24	450 - 500
15 - 19	400 - 440
0 - 15	270 - 390

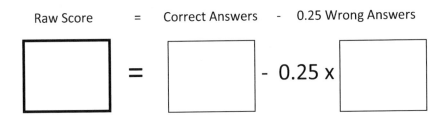

Raw Score   =   Correct Answers   -   0.25 Wrong Answers

$$\boxed{} = \boxed{} - 0.25 \times \boxed{}$$

Difficulty level

60 mins

<u>Question 1 -5</u> refer to the following choices:

(a)   Frequency

(b)   Pressure

(c)   Energy

(d)   Magnetic flux

(e)   Power

1.   N·m

2.   N m^{-2}

3.   V·s

4.   s^{-1}

5.   J s^{-1}

<u>Question 6 - 10</u> refer to the following law:

(a)   Law of conservation of energy

(b)   Law of conservation of momentum

(c)   Law of conservation of torque

(d)   Ohm's Law

(e)   Ideal gas law

6. Used to calculate volume of a heated balloon

7. Used to calculate velocity of a baseball after hit by a bat

8. To find height achieved by a ball thrown up vertically

9. Can be used to find the weight required to balance the see-saw

10. Is used to calculate the p.d. across a bulb

Question 11 - 15 use the following graph

a)

b)

c)

d)

e)

11. The graph of displacement versus time of a train moving at a constant velocity

12. The graph of speed versus time of a ball falling down to the ground

13. The graph of Boyle's law

14. The graph of horizontal velocity vs time of a projectile

15. The graph of p.d. vs current that of a filament bulb

16. How long approximately will it take an object of 5 kilogram to fall vertically down from a 50 meter tall building ?

a)   1.2 s

b)   1.6 s

c)   2.5 s

d)   3.2 s

e)   5.1 s

Question 17 - 19 use the information below:

A projectile is launched horizontally with a velocity of 30 m/s at the angle of 45°. Given that there is no air resistance.

17. How high will the object rise vertically ?

a)   10.6 m

b)   22.5 m

c)   30.7 m

d)   43.2 m

e)   59.1 m

18. How long does the journey take ?

a)   1.06 s

b)   2.12 s

c)   3.18 s

d)   4.24 s

e)   4.92 s

19. How far does the object travel horizontally?

a)   30 m

b)   45 m

c)   50 m

d)   75 m

e)   90 m

52 mins

Question 20 - 21 use the information below:

London-eye has a radius of 60 m took about 20 second to complete one revolution.

20. What is its angular velocity ?

a)   0.144 rad/s

b)   0.223 rad/s

c)   0.314 rad/s

d)   0.413 rad/s

e)   0.523 rad/s

21. What is the centripetal acceleration experienced by the passenger ?

a)   1.09 ms^{-2}

b)   2.51 ms^{-2}

c)   3.04 ms^{-2}

d)   4.32 ms^{-2}

e)   5.91 ms^{-2}

22. A system undergoes isothermal expansion, 150 J of heat is supplied to the system. How much work is done on the system that expand from 30 cm³ to 45 cm³ ?

a)   0   J

b)   75   J

c)   150 J

d)   300 J

e)   2250 J

Question 23 - 24

A canon-gun toy of mass 300g shoots a canon-ball of mass 20g out with a speed of 5m/s. Assuming there is no heat loss.

23. What is the recoil velocity of the canon ?

a)   0.33 m/s

b)   0.66 m/s

c)   1.33 m/s

d)   3.25 m/s

e)   5   m/s

24. If the gun and the ball were in contact for 0.02 second, then what is the force of impact on the ball ?

a)   5   N

b)   50   N

c)   500   N

d)   5000   N

e)   10000 N

25. Temperature of 50K is equivalent to

a)   323 °C

b)   223 °C

c)   50 °C

d)   -50 °C

e)   -223 °C

26. A D.J. at 60 cent club decided to raise the loudness of the sound up, which of the property(s) of sound wave changes?

a)   frequency

b)   amplitude

c)   quality

d)   pitch and quality

e)   amplitude and pitch

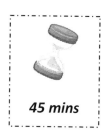

27. A uniform rod of mass 4 kilogram is in equilibrium due to the weight hung at point P. What is the value of the weight ?

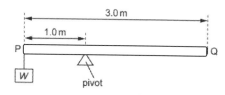

a)   10 N

b)   20 N

c)   30 N

d)   40 N

e)   80 N

28. Magnetic field will not have any effect on which particle ?

a)   proton

b)   electron

c)   photon

d)   alpha particles

e)   beta particles

29. An object that is white shinny are generally good

a)   absorber of heat

b)   refractor of heat

c)   reflector of heat

d)   radiator of heat

e)   all of the above

30. An object is placed 5 cm from the mirror, which of the following is the correct properties of the image produced ?

a) real and inverted

b) virtual and inverted

c) real and 5 cm away from the object

d) virtual and 5 cm away from the object

e) virtual and 10 cm away from the object

31. Which of the following wave would travel slowest in air ?

a)   sound wave

b)   infra-red

c)   radio wave

d)   beta ray

e)   gamma ray

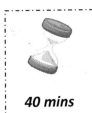

40 mins

A block of mass 0.5 kg is compressed against the spring with a spring constant of 3 N/m.

32. What is the frequency of the oscillation ?

a)   0.25   Hz

b)   0.39   Hz

c)   0.86   Hz

d)   1.79   Hz

e)   2.56   Hz

33. If the block is released from the spring after a compression of 10 cm at what velocity will it move ?

a)   9.2   cm/s

b)   10.0   cm/s

c)   12.5   cm/s

d)   21.4   cm/s

e)   24.5   cm/s

34. The block that was released collide with the black ball of mass 0.2kg, the speed of the block after collision is 8 cm/s. What is the velocity of the black ball ?

a)   21.4   cm/s

b)   24.5   cm/s

c)   32.3   cm/s

d)   37.1   cm/s

e)   41.3   cm/s

35. A bus starting from rest with a uniform acceleration of 8 m/s^2 for 5 seconds in a straight road would cover a distance of

a)   20   m

b)   40   m

c)   80   m

d)   100   m

e)   200   m

36. An object moving at constant speed will

a)   have no acceleration

b)   have a positive resultant force

c)   have a positive acceleration

d)   have a negative resultant force

e)   have a negative acceleration

Question 37 - 40 use below information

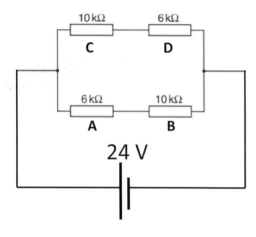

37. What is the total resistance of the circuit ?

a)   4   kΩ

b)   8   kΩ

c)   16   kΩ

d)   32   kΩ

e)   48   kΩ

38. What is the potential difference at resistor A ?

a)   9 V   b)   12 V

c)   15 V   d)   20 V

e)   24 V

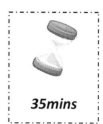

35mins

39. What is the power supply by the battery ?

a)   0.003   W

b)   0.012   W

c)   0.036   W

d)   0.048   W

e)   0.072   W

40. If we remove resistor A and C from the circuit what would the total resistance of the circuit be ?

a)   2.5   kΩ

b)   3.75   kΩ

c)   5.5   kΩ

d)   8.0   kΩ

e)   16.0   kΩ

41. In what way does isotopes of an atom differs from one another ?

a) different charges

b) different number of electrons

c) different number of neutrons

d) different number of protons

e) different number of photons

42. Which quantity would result from a calculation in which a potential difference is multiplied by an electric charge?

a) electric current

b) electric energy

c) electrical resistance

d) electric field strength

e) electric power

Question 43 - 45 use the information below

Visible light enters the glass that has a refractive index of 1.52

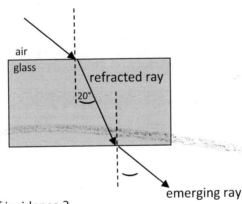

43. What is the angle of incidence ?

    a)   13.0°

    b)   24.3°

    c)   25.6°

    d)   31.3°

    e)   42.5°

44. What is the speed of light in this glass ?

    a) 1.97×10^8 m /s

    b) 2.32×10^8 m/s

    c) 3×10^8 m/s

    d) 4.56×10^8 m/s

    e) 5.06×10^8 m/s

45. What is the critical angle of glass block ?

    a)   23.0°

    b)   34.3°

    c)   35.6°

    d)   38.3°

    e)   41.1°

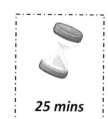

Question 46 - 48 use the graph below

Pressure(kPa)

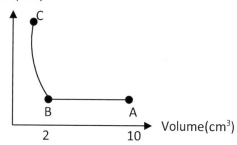

C

B   A

2   10   Volume(cm³)

46. A box contain air of volume 10 cm³ at 1 atm is compressed to 2 cm³. How much work is done in compressing the air ?

a)   0.65   J

b)   0.81   J

c)   3.50   J

d)   6.28   J

e)   8.00   J

47. What process is taking place from B to C ?

a)   Isothermal

b)   Isobaric

c)   Isochoric

d)   Adiabatic

e)   Radioactive

48. Given that from B to C work done in compressing the gas further is 0.35 J. What is the change in internal energy ?

a)   - 0.35   J

b)   - 1.00   J

c)   - 1.116 J

d)   0.85   J

e)   0.35   J

49. What does 'p' and 'q' measures ?

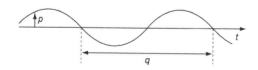

	p	q
a)	Amplitude	Period
b)	Amplitude	Wavelength
c)	Displacement	Period
d)	Displacement	Wavelength
e)	Amplitude	Frequency

50. How much energy is need to melt 500 grams of ice ?

a)   167   kJ

b)   334   kJ

c)   668   kJ

d)   986   kJ

e)   1670   kJ

SAT Physics Practice-Test

18 mins

51. A 20 W light bulb has a charge of 200C flows through it in 50 seconds time. What is the potential difference across the bulb ?

a) 0.4 V

b) 0.5 V

c) 4 V

d) 5 V

e) 10 V

52. Two silver wires A and B have the same area. Wire A is four times longer than wire B. What is the ratio of the resistance of wire B to wire A ?

a)   1/2

b)   1/4

c)   1/8

d)   2

e)   4

53. After an element A undergoes a beta decay, which of the following is true about its daughter nucleus ?

a) it loses one amu

b) it remains the same

c) it gains one amu

d) it loses two amu

e) it gains two amu

54. Which of the following is/are true about inelastic collision ?

(I)   momentum is conserved

(II)   kinetic energy is conserved

(III)   total energy is conserved

a)   (I) only

b)   (II) only

c)   (I) and (II)

d)   (I) and (III)

e)   (I) , (II) and (III)

55. Which word best describe H-2 and H-3 ?

a)   molecules

b)   cathode

c)   anode

d)   ions

e)   isotopes

56. Which of the following is used in time-delay circuit ?

a)   Diode

b)   Thermistor

c)   LDR

d)   LED

e)   Capacitor

57. Which of the following is not part of electromagnetic wave ?

a)   Infra-red rays

b)   Beta rays

c)   Gamma rays

d)   Radio wave

e)   X-rays

Question 58 - 60 use information below:

A wave moves thru double slit, given that distance between the slits are 5 cm and the distance from slit to the screen is 20 cm, while distance between the fringes are 2 cm.

58. What is the wavelength of this wave ?

a)   0.5   mm

b)   1.0   mm

c)   2.5   mm

d)   5.0   mm

e)   10   mm

12 mins

59. What is the distance from central maxima to second brightest fringe ?

a)   2   cm

b)   4   cm

c)   6   cm

d)   8   cm

e)   10   cm

60. If distance between the screen and the slit is double what is the distance between the fringes ?

a)   1   cm

b)   2   cm

c)   3   cm

d)   4   cm

e)   5   cm

61. Greatest constructive interference occurs when two waves are having a phase difference of

a)   30°

b)   90°

c)   180°

d)   270°

e)   360°

Question 62 - 64 use the following information:

Photoelectric effect graph

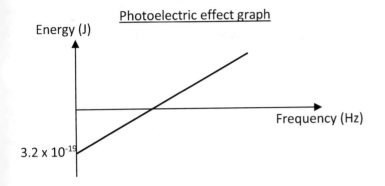

62. What is the threshold frequency ?

a)   4.83 x 10^{14} Hz

b)   3.24 x 10^{14} Hz

c)   3.05 x 10^{14} Hz

d)   2.07 x 10^{14} Hz

e)   1.53 x 10^{14} Hz

63. What is the maximum kinetic energy of photoelectron if the electromagnetic wave incidence has a wavelength of 420 nm ?

a)   3.24 x 10^{-19} J

b)   3.05 x 10^{-19} J

c)   2.07 x 10^{-19} J

d)   1.53 x 10^{-19} J

e)   1.07 x 10^{-19} J

64. According to question 63 ,what is the speed of emitted photoelectron?

a)   5.81 x 10^5 m/s

b)   6.12 x 10^5 m/s

c)   8.91 x 10^5 m/s

d)   2.31 x 10^6 m/s

e)   3.00 x 10^8 m/s

65. What is the period of a wave with a frequency of 5 GHz ?

a)   2   ns

b)   20   ns

c)   200   ps

d)   2000   μs

e)   20000 μs

66. One electron-Volt is equivalent to

a)   1.6 x 10^{19} J

b)   1.6 x 10^{-19} J

c)   9.11 x 10^{31} J

d)   9.11 x 10^{-31} J

e)   6.63 x 10^{-34} J

5 mins

Question 67 - 69 use the information below:

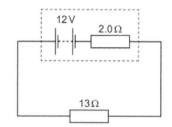

A cell has an e.m.f. of 12 volt is connected to a 13 ohms resistor. The cell has an internal resistance of 2 ohms.

67. What is the potential difference through 13 Ω resistor?

a)   1.6   V

b)   2.4   V

c)   6.0   V

d)   10.4   V

e)   12.0   V

68. What is the rate of energy used by the 13Ω resistor ?

a)   12   W

b)   9.60   W

c)   8.32   W

d)   5.40   W

e)   1.28   W

69. How much power is loss ?

a)   12   W

b)   9.60   W

c)   8.32   W

d)   5.40   W

e)   1.28   W

70. If a metal ring is heated then which of the following quantity would decreases ?

a)   density

b)   diameter

c)   thickness

d)   brightness

e)   volume

71. How many electrons orbit the hydrogen isotopes H-3 ?

a)   0

b)   1

c)   2

d)   3

e)   4

Question 72 - 75 refer to the diagram below:

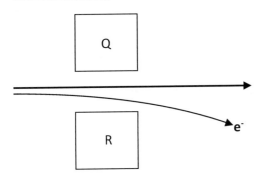

2 mins

Two rays pass through a region of electric field Q-R. One is unknown and another is a ray composed of a high speed electron.

72. Which kind of radiation is ray that deflect towards the pole R ?

a)   alpha

b)   beta

c)   x-rays

d)   gamma

e)   electromagnetic ray

73. Which kind of radiation is the ray that moves thru without any deflection called ?

a)   alpha

b)   beta

c)   proton beam

d)   gamma

e)   cathode ray

74. Which of the following statement is true ?

a)   Pole 'R' is positively charged

b)   Pole 'R' is negatively charged

c)   Pole 'Q' is negatively charged

d)   Pole 'Q' has no charge

e)   Pole ' Q' and 'R' have the same charge

75. What change would take place(if any) if we shoot a positron through the region instead of an electron ?

a)   no change

b)   more deflection in same direction

c)   no deflection occur

d)   same deflection in opposite direction

e)   more deflection in opposite direction

Question	Answer	Explanation
1.	C	Nm $\rightarrow$ force x distance = Work or Energy
2.	B	Nm^{-2} $\rightarrow$ force ÷ area = Pressure
3.	D	Vs $\rightarrow$ p.d. x time = Magnetic ux
4.	A	s^{-1} $\rightarrow$ 1/Time = Frequency
5.	E	Js^{-1} $\rightarrow$ energy ÷ time = Power
6.	E	We can apply the concept of ideal gas here $$V_1 : T_1 = V_2 : T_2$$
7.	B	Using law of conservation of momentum $$m_1u_1 + m_2u_2 = m_1v_1 + m_2v_2$$
8.	A	We can use law of conservation of energy here $$KE = PE$$
9.	C	Turning effect of force in equilibrium can be view as $$\text{Total clockwise torque} = \text{Total anti-clockwise torque}$$
10.	D	Ohm's Law can be used to help calculate the p.d. $$V = IR$$
11.	B	The graph of displacement vs time of an object moving at a constant velocity means that we can view this as a directly proportional graph As time increases the displacement also increases
12.	B	As the ball fall its velocity is zero (starts from rest) then velocity is incresing due to the effect of gravity. We can say graph of speed vs time is directly proportional
13.	E	Boyle's law say Presurre is inversly proportional to volume
14.	A	Horizontal velocity of a projectile always remain constant
15.	D	The graph is almost directly proportional, except that filament bulb produces heat so its going to curve due to heat loss

Question	Answer	Explanation
16.	D	$Y = ut + 0.5\,at^2$ $50 = 0(t) + 0.5\,(10)\,t^2$ $T = 3.16 \approx 3.2$ sec
17.	B	$V^2 = U^2 + 2\,a\,s$ $0^2 = (30\sin45)^2 + 2\,(10)\,s$ $s = 22.5$ m
18.	D	$T_{up} = V_i \sin\theta \div g$ $T_{up} = 30\sin45 \div g$ $T_{up} = 2.12$ s $T_{down} = T_{up}$ Total time $= T_{up} + T_{down}$ Total time $= 2.12 + 2.12 = 4.24$ second
19.	E	Range $= V_i \cos\theta \times 2\,t_{up}$ Range $= 30\cos45 \times 2(2.12)$ Range $= 90$ meter
20.	C	$\omega = \Delta\theta \div \Delta t$ $\omega = 2\pi \div 20$ $\omega = 0.314$ rad/s
21.	E	$a_c = r \times \omega^2 = 60 \times (0.314)^2 = 5.91\ ms^{-2}$
22.	C	During isothermal expansion $\Delta U \to Q = W$ $Q = 150$ J $W = 150$ Joules
23.	A	total momentum before = total momentum after $0 = 300(v) + 20(5)$ $v = 0.333$ m/s
24.	A	$\Delta P = m\,\Delta v$ $F\Delta t = 0.02\,(5 - 0)$ $F \times 0.02 = 0.1$ $F = 5$ N
25.	E	$T_c = T_k - 273$ $T_c = 50 - 273 = -223\,^{\circ}C$
26.	B	Loudness of sound depend mainly on the amplitude

Question	Answer	Explanation
27.	B	In equilibrium Total clockwise torque $\quad=$ Total anti-clockwise torque Weight of rod x D_1 $\quad=\quad$ W x D_2 $40 \times 0.5 \quad\quad=\quad$ W x 1 W $\quad\quad\quad\quad=\quad$ 20 N
28.	C	A photon has no mass and no charge, therefore it will not experience any field effect.
29.	C	White shinny object are a good reflector of heat radiation, since white is the color that absorb very little heat.
30.	E	An object 5 cm from the mirror will have a virtual image of 5 cm inside the mirror. So we can say that the image is virtual and 10cm away from the object.
31.	A	Choice b,c and e are electromagnetic wave which travels at the speed of light Choice d travels nearly equal to speed of light Sound wave would travel slowest (330 m/s)
32.	B	We can find period first by using $$T = 2\pi\sqrt{\frac{m}{k}} = 2\pi\sqrt{\frac{0.5}{3}} = 2.56 \text{ sec}$$ We want the frequency so $$F = \frac{1}{T} = \frac{1}{2.56} = 0.39 \text{ Hz}$$
33.	E	Elastic PE $\quad=\quad$ Kinetic enegy $0.5\ k\ x^2 \quad=\quad 0.5\ m\ v^2$ $(3)(10/100)^2 = \quad (0.5)\ v^2$ v $\quad\quad=\quad$ 24.5 cm/s
34.	E	Total momentum before $\quad=\quad$ Total momentum after $(0.5)(24.5) \quad\quad=\quad (0.5)(8) + 0.2\ (v)$ v $\quad\quad\quad=\quad$ 41.3 m/s
35.	D	We can use equation of motion here $s = u\ t + 0.5\ a\ t^2$ $s = (0)(5) + 0.5(8)(5)^2$ $s = 100 \text{ m}$
36.	A	Constant speed means that the acceleration is equal to zero

Question	Answer	Explanation
37.	B	$R_{AB} = R_A + R_B = 6k + 10k = 16\ k\Omega$ $R_{CD} = R_C + R_D = 10k + 6k = 16\ k\Omega$ $1/R_{total} = 1/R_{AB} + 1/R_{CD}$ $1/R_{total} = 1/16 + 1/16$ $R_{total} = 8\ k\Omega$
38.	B	$V_A = R_A \times V_{total} / R_{AB}$ $V_A = 6 \times 24 / 16$ $V_A = 9\ V$
39.	E	$I_{total} = V_{total} / R_{total}$ $I_{total} = 24 / (8 \times 10^3)$ $I_{total} = 0.003\ A$ $P_{supply} = I_{total} \times V_{total}$ $P_{supply} = 0.003 \times 24$ $P_{supply} = 0.072\ W$
40.	B	So only D and B is left **6 kΩ** **10 kΩ** $1/R_{total} = 1/6 + 1/10$ $R_{total} = 3.75\ k\Omega$
41.	C	Isotopes of an atom would have the same number of protons but different number of neutrons
42.	B	If we multiply $V \times Q \rightarrow (I\ R) \times (I\ T)$ $I^2\ R \times T = $ Power x Time = Energy
43.	D	$n_{air}\ \sin\theta_i = n_{glass}\ \sin\theta_r$ $1 \times \sin\theta_i = 1.52\ \sin20$ $\theta_i = 31.3°$
44.	A	*Air*　　　　*Glass* $n_1\ v_1 = n_2\ v_2$ $1 \times (3.10^8) = 1.52 \times V$ $V = 1.97 \times 10^8\ m/s$
45.	E	$n = 1/\sin\theta_c$ $\theta_c = \sin^{-1}(1/n)$ $\theta_c = 41.1°$

Question	Answer	Explanation
46.	B	Work = P x ΔV Work = $(101 \times 10^3) \times [(10-2) \times 10^{-6}]$ Work = 0.81 J
47.	D	The process from B to C is known as adiabatic compression Because no heat was added to the system
48.	A	The process from B to C is adiabatic which means Q = 0 So we apply law of thermodynamic $Q = \Delta U + W$ $0 = \Delta U + 0.35$ $\Delta U = -0.35$ J
49.	C	'p' is not the amplitude it is the displacement of the wave 'q' is the time period of wave
50.	A	We use $Q = m\, H_v$ $= 0.5 \times 334$ kJ/kg $= 167$ kJ
51.	D	We want to find p.d. V We first find I by using $I = \Delta Q \div \Delta T$ we get $I = 200 \div 50 = 4$ A Then we use $P = I V$ $20 = 4 (V)$ $V = 5$ volt
52.	B	To find $R_B : R_A \rightarrow$ We refer to R is directly proportional to L $R_A / L_A = R_B / L_B$ $R_A / 4L_B = R_B / L_B$ $L_B / 4L_B = R_B / R_A$ $R_B : R_A = 1:4$ $R_B : R_A = 1/4$
53.	C	After lossing an electron element A will have +1 to its proton number This increases the amu by 1
54.	D	During an inelastic collision a momentum is conserved but kinetic energy is not Keep in mind that total energy is always conserved, some energy during the collision turned into heat and sound during the impact.
55.	E	Isotopes are shown here since H-2 and H-3 has same number of proton but different number of neutrons

Question	Answer	Explanation
56.	E	In a time-delay circuit we have to use capacitor because we want it to be fully charged first then it wil give discharge , allowing current to flow in the circuit.
57.	B	All of the following are part of EM except Beta rays Beta is made of a high speed electron
58.	D	$\frac{\lambda}{d} = \frac{x}{L} \rightarrow \frac{\lambda}{5} = \frac{2}{20}$ $\lambda = 0.5$ cm or 5 mm
59.	B	From $n = 0$ to $n = 2 \rightarrow N = 2$ We can use $N \cdot x = 2 \cdot 2 = 4$ cm
60.	D	Distance L is directly proportional to fringe x We can say $L_1 / x_1 = L_2 / x_2 \rightarrow 20/2 = 40/x_2$ $x_2 = 4$ cm
61.	E	Greatest or maximum constructive interference occurs when two waves are inphase or phase difference is 0 or 360°
62.	A	To find threshold frequency we set $E_k = 0$ $E_k = hf - \Phi$ $0 = (6.63 \times 10^{-34}) f - 3.2 \times 10^{-19}$ $f = 4.83 \times 10^{14}$ Hz
63.	D	$E_k = hf - \Phi$ $E_k = (6.63 \times 10^{-34})(3 \times 10^8)/(420 \times 10^{-9}) - 3.2 \times 10^{-19}$ $E_k = 1.53 \times 10^{-19}$ J
64.	A	$E_k = 1/2\, m\, v^2$ $V_{electron} = (2 \times E_k / m_{electron})^{1/2}$ $V_{electron} = 580645 = 5.81 \times 10^5$ m/s
65.	C	Frequency = 1/ period Period = 1/ frequency Period = $1/(5 \times 10^9) = 2 \times 10^{-10}$ s or 200 ps
66.	B	1 eV = 1.6×10^{-19} J

Question	Answer	Explanation
67.	D	We apply Ohm's Law by adding the two resistor in series → R_T = 2 + 13 = 15 Ω $$V_T = I_T R_T$$ $$12 = I_T \times 15$$ $$I_T = 0.8 \text{ A}$$ $$V_R = I_T \times R = 0.8 \times 13 = 10.4 \text{ V}$$
68.	C	To find rate of energy or power used by the resistor we use $$P = I^2 \times R$$ $$P = 0.8^2 \times 13$$ $$P = 8.32 \text{ w}$$
69.	E	To find rate of energy loss we calculate power loss in internal resistor $$P = I^2 \times r$$ $$P = 0.8^2 \times 2$$ $$P = 1.28 \text{ w}$$
70.	A	When we heat an object it would expand, which means more volume Volume is inversely proportional to density → $D = \dfrac{m}{v}$ → more 'v' means less 'D' So density decreases.
71.	B	Isotopes have same number of proton(s) Hydrogen have only 1 proton which means there exist only 1 electron in the orbital shell
72.	B	Beta particles are made of electrons that are moving in high speed
73.	D	Gamma rays are electromagnetic waves that experienced no effect on electric field
74.	A	By looking at the path that electron beam moves we can conclude that 'R' must be postively charged
75.	D	Positrons are postively charged particles which have similar mass to electrons, therefore it would deflect in the same manner but in the opposite direction

Score Range

Raw Score	Conversion
65 - 75	800
59 - 64	750 - 790
53 - 58	720 - 740
48 - 52	690 - 710
42 - 47	650 - 680
36 - 41	590 - 640
30 - 35	540 - 580
25 - 29	510 - 530
20 - 24	450 - 500
15 - 19	400 - 440
0 - 15	270 - 390

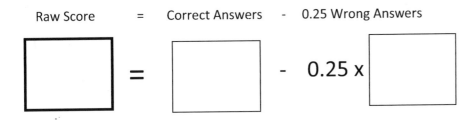

Raw Score = Correct Answers - 0.25 Wrong Answers

$$\boxed{} = \boxed{} - 0.25 \times \boxed{}$$

Practice Test 2

Question 1 -5 <u>refer to the following choices:</u>

(a)   Specific Heat Capacity

(b)   Heat Capacity

(c)   Power

(d)   Latent heat of fusion

(e)   None of the above

The units below belong to which quantity

1. $J \cdot K^{-1}$

2. $N \cdot m \cdot s^{-1}$

3. $J \cdot kg^{-1}$

4. $J \cdot kg$

5. $J \, (kg \, °c)^{-1}$

<u>Question 6 - 10</u> refer to the following:

(a)   stay the same

(b)   halved

(c)   doubled

(d)   quartered

(e)   quadrupled

6. The diameter of a wire is doubled, what happen to the resistance ?

7. Height of the balloon is increased by four times, what happen to its gravitational potential energy ?

8. A box of gas is heated so its volume doubled, what happen to the mass of gas ?

9. If the p.d. across a bulb is doubled, what happen to the current in the bulb ?

10. The orbital radius of a planet from the Sun is doubled, what happen to the orbital speed ?

Question 11 - 15 use the information below:

a)   James Watt

b)   Galileo Galilei

c)   Isaac Newton

d)   Michael Faraday

e)   Albert Einstein

Match the scientist to the following question

11. Discovered that mass can be converted into energy and vice versa

12. Discovered the concept of electromagnetic induction

13. Discovered that an object drop from the same altitude will fall with the same acceleration

14. Discovered that two bodies in space will attract one another

15. Developed the idea of power

Question 16 - 17 use the information below:

A bus travelling with a speed of 30 m/s slows down to a bus stop over a distance of 200m

16. How long does it take the bus to stop ?

a)   3.2   s

b)   4.6   s

c)   6.7   s

d)   11.2 s

e)   13.3 s

17. What is the average deceleration of the bus?

a)   1.2 ms^{-2}

b)   1.6 ms^{-2}

c)   2.3 ms^{-2}

d)   3.2 ms^{-2}

e)   5.1 ms^{-2}

Question 18 - 20 use the information below:

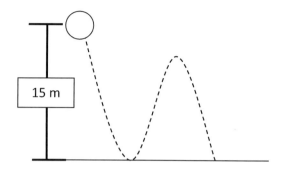

15 m

18. A 500 g ball is dropped from the height of 15 m. If energy loss is 20% on each bounce, how high will the first bounce be ?

a)   14 m

b)   12 m

c)   10 m

d)   6 m

e)   3 m

19. What is the velocity of the first bounce ?

a)   15.5   m/s

b)   12.2   m/s

c)   9.8   m/s

d)   7.4   m/s

e)   6.0   m/ s

20. What is the impulse deliver to the ball on the first bounce ?

a)   23.2   kg·m/s

b)   16.4   kg·m/s

c)   8.25   kg·m/s

d)   1.65   kg·m/s

e)   0.90   kg·m/s

21. Electric field will not have any effect on which particle ?

a)   proton

b)   electron

c)   photon

d)   alpha particles

e)   beta particles

22. An object that is dull black are generally good

a)   absorber of heat

b)   refractor of heat

c)   reflector of heat

d)   diffractor of heat

e)   all of the above

SAT Physics Practice-Test

Question 23 - 25 use the information below:

A monochromatic light enters the water with the angle of incidence of 35 degree, the refractive index of water is 1.33

23. What is the speed of this light in the water ?

a) 3.99×10^8 m/s

b) 3.0×10^8 m/s

c) 2.25×10^8 m/s

d) 1.93×10^8 m/s

e) 1.33×10^8 m/s

24. What is the critical angle of the water ?

a)   48.8 °

b)   38.5 °

c)   25.5 °

d)   21.8 °

e)   19.2 °

25. What property of light would remain the same when it enters the water?

a)   wavelength

b)   amplitude

c)   velocity

d)   speed

e)   frequency

26. Which of the following graph of R vs V show a property of an ohmic conductor ?

a)

b)

c)

d)

e)

SAT Physics Practice-Test

27. Which statement about alpha radiation is TRUE ?

a)   It is an electromagnetic wave

b)   It is more penetrating than gamma ray

c)   It is a stream of fast-moving electrons

d)   It has more ionising effect than beta

e)   It is a composed of hydrogen atom

28. Temperature of -20°C is equivalent to

a)   293 K

b)   273 K

c)   253 K

d)   -253 K

e)   -293 K

Use the information below for question 29-30

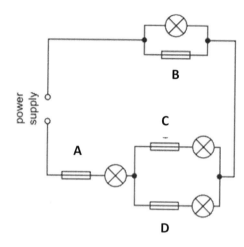

29. One of the fuse blow up, so none of the lamp is on. Which fuse blow up?

a)   A

b)   B

c)   C

d)   B and C

e)   B and D

30. If each bulb has a resistance of 10Ω, then what is the total resistance of the circuit ?

a)   60 Ω

b)   45 Ω

c)   40 Ω

d)   25 Ω

e)   20 Ω

31. Which of the following is the best way to find lower fixed point of a thermometer ?

a)   put thermometer in boiling water

b)   compare it with other thermometer

c)   mark the lowest part of the liquid

d)   put thermometer in melting ice

e)   put thermometer in freezer

32. An object placed 3 cm from a convex lens whose focal length is 2 cm will be have a magnification factor of

a)   3

b)   2

c)   1.5

d)   1

e)   0

33. According to question 32 which of the following show the properties of the image ?

a)   diminished and virtual

b)   diminished and real

c)   magnified and virtual

d)   magnified and real

e)   inverted and virtual

34. Which of the following is NOT TRUE about an object moving at constant speed around a circular track ?

a)   it has zero acceleration

b)   there is a friction between object and the track

c)   it will have an acceleration towards the center of the track

d)   it will leave the track soon if frictional force is decreased

e)   there is a centripetal force

35. Which of the following energy resource generates electricity without using any moving parts ?

a)   tidal wave

b)   geothermal

c)   nuclear

d)   hydroelectric

e)   solar

36. Three-million micrometer is equivalent to

a)   0.3   m

b)   3   m

c)   30   m

d)   300   m

e)   30,000 m

Question 37 - 40 use the following information:

200 N

θ

Frictional force between the box and the floor is 100 N.

37. At what angle must the force be applied so that the box move at constant velocity ?

a)   60°

b)   45°

c)   30°

d)   15°

e)   5°

38. If the coefficient of friction between the box and the floor is 0.4, then what is the mass of the box ?

a)   55.1   kg

b)   42.3   kg

c)   25.0   kg

d)   20.0   kg

e)   18.7   kg

39. If the box moved a distance of 3 meter, how much work is done against friction ?

a)   600   J

b)   500   J

c)   400   J

d)   300   J

e)   150   J

40. Assuming that the temperature between the floor and the box increased by 20°c. What is the thermal capacity of the box in J/°c ?

a)   25

b)   20

c)   15

d)   10

e)   5

41. Which quantity is conserved during collisions between atoms ?

a) Kinetic energy

b) Momentum

c) Momentum and Kinetic energy

d) Momentum and Potential energy

e) Kinetic energy and Potential energy

SAT Physics Practice-Test

42. Which of the following is quantity of e.m.f ?

a) coulomb per second

b) coulomb per joules

c) ampere per second

d) joules per second

e) joules per coulomb

43. What is the mass left over of a 300g radioactive substance ,whose half-life is 9 days, after 45 days ?

a)   60.0   g

b)   45.5   g

c)   32.5   g

d)   19.3   g

e)   9.4   g

44. Which of the following particles listed below is positively charged and lightest ?

a)   Proton

b)   Positron

c)   Electron

d)   Nucleus

e)   Neutron

Question 45 - 46 use the graph below

30 mins

Pressure(MPa)

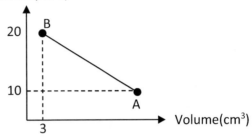

45. How much work is done in compressing the gas in the box from A to B?

a)   3   J

b)   6   J

c)   30   J

d)   45   J

e)   70   J

46. What process is taking place from A to B ?

a)   Isothermal contraction

b)   Isobaric contraction

c)   Isochoric contraction

d)   Isothermal expansion

e)   Isobaric expansion

SAT Physics Practice-Test

47. Which of the following shows an electric field around a negative charge ?

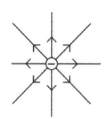

a)

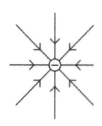

b)

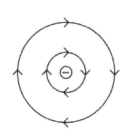

c)

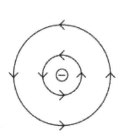

d)

e) none of the above

48. Which of the following may produce a stationary wave ?

a) water moving through a narrow slit

b) making a loud sound near a mountain

c) blowing air over at the top of an empty bottle

d) passing monochromatic light through double slit

e) shooting light in the fiber optic

49. Which device's resistance varies inversely as temperature change?

a)   LDR

b)   Diode

c)   LED

d)   Thermistor

e)   Rheostat

50. One-thousand kilogram cannon shoots a cannon ball of mass ten kilogram with a velocity of 150 m/s. What is the recoil velocity ?

a)   0.15   m/s

b)   1.5   m/s

c)   3.0   m/s

d)   15   m/s

e)   30   m/s

51. What is the maximum height reached by a stone thrown up with a vertical velocity of 16 m/s ?

a)   25.6   m

b)   12.8   m

c)   6.4   m

d)   3.2   m

e)   1.6   m

52. A disc spin at the rate of 50 revolution per minutes, what is the angular velocity of the disc in rad/s ?

a) 15.3

b) 7.43

c) 5.23

d) 1.67

e) 0.83

53. What is the ratio of intensity of sound heard by the person that is 5 meter away to 10 meters away ?

a)   1 : 2

b)   1 : 4

c)   1 : 5

d)   2 : 1

e)   4 : 1

54. Which of the following electromagnetic wave has the highest energy ?

a)   Infra-red rays

b)   Beta rays

c)   UV rays

d)   Radio wave

e)   X-rays

55. A 1000 kg car travels forward at the speed of 25 m/s and then backward at the velocity of 10 m/s. What is the change in kinetic energy of the car ?

a)   100.5   kJ

b)   112.5   kJ

c)   225.5   kJ

d)   262.5   kJ

e)   325.5   kJ

56. Which quantity remains constant as the ball falls from the top of the building to the ground?

a)   speed

b)   velocity

c)   air resistance

d)   acceleration

e)   drag force

57. A monochromatic light illuminates two narrow slits, the interference pattern results is seen on the screen some distance beyond the slits. Which change increases the separation between the dark lines of the interference pattern ?

a) using monochromatic light of higher frequency

b) using monochromatic light of lower frequency

c) decreasing the distance between the screen and the slits

d) increasing the distance between the slits

e) decreasing the thickness of the slit

Question 58 - 60 use information below:

A projectile is launched horizontally with a velocity of 30 m/s above the ground, at the altitude of 500 meter. Ignoring air resistance.

58. How long does it take the projectile to hit the ground ?

a)   5   s

b)   10   s

c)   12.5   s

d)   16.6   s

e)   18.2   s

59. What is the horizontal distance travel ?

a)   300   m

b)   375   m

c)   426   m

d)   498   m

e)   546   m

60. At t = 2 seconds what is the velocity of the object ?

a)   20   m/s

b)   25.6   m/s

c)   30   m/s

d)   36   m/s

e)   43.2   m/s

61. Greatest destructive interference occurs when two waves are having a phase difference of

a)   30°

b)   90°

c)   180°

d)   270°

e)   360°

62. Which of the following particles a has the greatest momentum ? Given that all are moving with a same initial velocity.

a) Alpha particles

b) Protons

c) Neutrons

d) Electrons

e) Positron

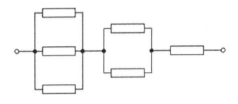

65. Each resistor above has a resistance of R and a combined resistance of 66 Ω. What is the value of R ?

a)   11   Ω

b)   15   Ω

c)   18   Ω

d)   22   Ω

e)   36   Ω

63. Which of the following is surely to create a beat ?

a)   sound waves with difference amplitude

b)   sound waves with difference loudness

c)   sound waves with difference source

d)   sound waves with difference pitch

e)   sound waves that produce echo

66. In which of the following will there be no polarization ?

a)   Light waves being scattered

b)   Light wave being reflected

c)   Sound waves passing through a grid

d)   Microwaves passing through a grid

e)   UV passing through a translucent glass

64. What is the wavelength of an electromagnetic wave with a frequency of 6GHz ?

a)   0.5   cm

b)   5   cm

c)   50   cm

d)   500   cm

e)   5000   cm

67. If hot water cools then which of the following property would increases ?

a)   density of water

b)   mass of water

c)   number of molecules

d)   distance between molecules

e)   volume of water

68. How many electrons are orbiting the alpha particle emitted out by a radioactive isotope?

a)   0

b)   1

c)   2

d)   3

e)   4

69. If 300 coulomb of charges pass through a wire per minute then how much current is running through the wire ?

a)   5   A

b)   10   A

c)   50   A

d)   100   A

e)   300   A

70. Which of the following is NOT TRUE about evaporation ?

a) involve change of phase

b) occurs at a fix temperature

c) causing reduction in average kinetic energy of molecules

d) does not necessary occur at a boiling point

e) require external heat energy

71. Which kind of radiation can be stop by a cloth ?

a)   alpha

b)   beta

c)   infra-red ray

d)   gamma

e)   cathode ray

72. Which of the following statement is TRUE about Einstein law of relativity?

a) Speed of light in vacuum can varies

b) A proton can travel at the speed of light

c) Electrons can move faster than light

d) Gravity has no effect on the speed of light

e) Neutron can move at the speed of light

Question 73 - 75 use the below information:

An electromagnetic wave incidents on a metal whose work function is 3.2 x 10⁻¹⁹ J, this result in an emission of a photo-electron whose kinetic energy is 3.43 x 10⁻¹⁹ J.

73. What change is required in order to increase number of emitted electrons ?

a) change the type of metal

b) use low-frequency electromagnetic wave

c) use a monochromatic light

d) increase intensity of light

e) increase frequency of incident ray

75. What is approximate velocity of emitted photo-electron ?

a)   6.14 x 10⁵   m/s

b)   8.39 x 10⁵   m/s

c)   8.68 x 10⁵   m/s

d)   1.21 x 10⁶   m/s

e)   1.52 x 10⁶   m/s

74. What was the frequency of incident electromagnetic wave ?

a)   4.82 x 10¹⁴   Hz

b)   5.17 x 10¹⁴   Hz

c)   1.0 x 10¹⁵   Hz

d)   4.82 x 10¹⁵   Hz

e)   5.17 x 10¹⁵   Hz

Answer Key 2

Question	Answer	Explanation
1.	B	JK^{-1} → heat ÷ change in temperature = heat capacity
2.	C	$N \cdot m \cdot s^{-1}$ → force x distance ÷ time = Work ÷ time = Power
3.	D	$J \cdot kg^{-1}$ → energy ÷ mass = latent heat of fusion
4.	E	$J \cdot kg$ → energy x mass = none of the above
5.	A	$J\,(kg\,°c)^{-1}$ → energy ÷ (mass x change in temperature) = Speci c heat capacity
6.	D	We can apply the concept of R is inversely proportional to area $R_1\,x\,A_1 \quad = \quad R_2\,x\,A_2$ $r\,x\,(\pi\,1^2) \quad = \quad R_2\,x\,(\pi\,2^2)$ $R_2 \quad\quad = \quad r/4$ The new resistance is quartered of the old one
7.	E	We know that $\quad GPE = m\,g\,h \quad$ (GPE is directly proportional to 'h') So if 'h' is increased by 4 times → GPE will also increased by 4 times
8.	A	According to gas law mass is always fixed, no matter what happen to volume, temperature or pressure. So no change in mass
9.	C	Ohm's Law can be used here $V = I\,R,$ where R remains constant So we can say V is directly proportional to I If V is doulbed then 'I' will also double.
10.	B	According to angular momentum $\Delta L \quad = \quad mvr$ $m_1\,v_1\,r_1 \;=\; m_2\,v_2\,r_2$ $m\,v_1\,R \;=\; m\,v_2\,(2R)$ $v_2 \;=\; v_1/2$ Therefore the new velocity will be halved
11.	E	$E = mc^2$ → This law is discovered by Albert Einstein
12.	D	e.m.f. $= \Delta\Phi\,/\,\Delta t$ → Concept of electromagnetic induction is discovered by Michael Faraday

SAT Physics Practice-Test

Question	Answer	Explanation
13.	B	$a_g = 9.8$ m/s^2 on every object $\rightarrow$ This is discovered by Galileo Galilei
14.	C	$F_g = G\, m_1 m_2 \div R^2 \rightarrow$ This law is discovered by Isaac Newton
15.	A	Power is rate of work $\rightarrow$ This is discovered by James Watt
16.	E	We use equation of motions here S = 200 m U = 0 V = 30 m/s T = ?? $$S = \frac{(V+U)\,T}{2}$$ $$T = \frac{2 \times S}{(V+U)} = \frac{2 \times 200}{(30+0)} = 13.3 \text{ seconds}$$
17.	C	We use equation of motions here S = 200 m U = 0 V = 30 m/s a = ?? $$V^2 = U^2 + 2aS \rightarrow 30^2 = 0^2 + 2a(200)$$ $$a = 2.25 \approx 2.3 \text{ m/s}^2$$
18.	B	Energy loss by 20% means only 80% left. $GPE_2 = 0.8\, GPE_1$ $m\,g\,h_2 = 0.8\, m\,g\,h_1$ $h_2 = 0.8\,(15)$ $h_2 = 12$ m
19.	A	We use law of conservation of energy $GPE_2 = KE_2$ $mgh = 0.5\, m\, v^2$ $gh = 0.5\, v^2$ $v^2 = 2 \times g \times h$ $v^2 = 2 \times 10 \times 12$ $v = 15.5$ m/s

Question	Answer	Explanation
20.	B	Impluse $\rightarrow \Delta p = m \, \Delta v = m \, (V_f - V_i)$ We need $V_i \rightarrow$ GPE = KE $mgh = 0.5 \, mv_i^2$ $2 \times 10 \, (15) = v_i^2$ $v_i = 17.3$ m/s $\Delta p = m \, (V_f - V_i) = 0.5 \, (15.5 - (-17.3)) = 16.4$ kg·m/s
21.	C	A photon has no mass and no charge, therefore it will not experience any field effect.
22.	A	Dull black object are a good absorber of heat radiation, since black is the color that absorb most heat ray.
23.	C	$n = \dfrac{V_{air}}{V_{water}} \rightarrow V_{water} = \dfrac{V_{air}}{n} = \dfrac{3 \times 10^8}{1.33} = 2.25 \times 10^8$ m/s
24.	A	$n = \dfrac{1}{\sin (C)} \rightarrow \sin (C) = \dfrac{1}{n} = \dfrac{1}{1.33}$ $C = 48.8\,°$
25.	E	When light enters a different medium only wavelength changes, frequency remians the same
26.	A	As p.d. changes the value of R remains constant, since this is an Ohmic conductor.
27.	D	Alpha has the most ionsing effect compare with beta and gamma
28.	C	To convert degree to Kelvin we add 273 to degree $-20 + 273 = 253$ K
29.	A	If bulb A breaks current cannot flow back so this act like an open switch in the circuit
30.	D	Bulb A and B are in series $\rightarrow R_{AB} = 10 + 10 = 20 \; \Omega$ Bulb C and D are in parallel $\rightarrow R_{CD} = 1/ \, (\, 1/10 + 1/10) = 5 \; \Omega$ Total resistance $= R_{AB} + R_{CD} = 25 \; \Omega$

Question	Answer	Explanation
31.	D	Lower fixed point is at $0°$ C To find lower fixed point we put the thermometer in melting ice, since ice melt at $0°$ C
32.	B	$1/f = 1/d_o + 1/d_i$ $1/2 = 1/3 + 1/d_i$ $d_i = 6$ cm $M = d_i / d_o$ $M = 6 / 3$ $M = 2$
33.	D	In convex lens if object is placed between F_1 and F_2 the image produced will be **real ,inverted** and magnified
34.	A	Object moving in circle will experienced a centripetal force, which means there is also a centripetal acceleration. Therefore it cannot have zero acceleration
35.	E	Energy generated with no moving parts must only be produced by a solar panel, so only possibility here would be 'solar' energy
36.	B	$3{,}000{,}000\ \mu m = 3 \times 10^6 \times 10^{-6}$ m $= 3$ m
37.	A	$\int = F \cos\theta$ $100 = 200 \cos\theta$ $\cos\theta = 0.5$ $\theta = 60°$
38.	B	 $N + F\sin\theta = mg$ $100/0.4 + 200\sin60 = m(10)$ $m = 42.3$ kg
39.	D	$W_f = \int \times d = 100 \times 3 = 300$ Joules

Question	Answer	Explanation
40.	B	Work against friction is considered to become heat energy so heat loss – 300 J Thermal capacity = Heat loss / change in temperature Thermal capacity = 300 / 20 = 15 J/°C
41.	C	Atomic collision are considered to be perfectly elastic. Therefore both the kinetic energy and the momentum are conserved
42.	E	We know that $U = qV$ $V = U/q$ So we can say 1 volt = 1 J/C
43.	E	Half-life is 9 days, so 45 days means n = 5 (half-life) Mass left over = $\dfrac{300}{2^5}$ = 9.375 ≈ 9.4 g
44.	B	Positively charged and lightest would be anti-electron or positron
45.	D	at A at B $P_1 V_1$ = $P_2 V_2$ 20 x 3 = 10 x V_2 V_2 = 6 cm^3 To find work done we must find area under the graph Work = Area = 1/2 (3) (10 + 20) = 45 J
46.	A	If we are using $P_1 V_1 = P_2 V_2$, then we must fixed temperature and mass This means no change in temperature and the volume reduces, therefore this is considered to be 'Isothermal contration'
47.	B	The electric field around a charge will point inward to the surface of the charge
48.	C	The wave produce by blowing into a bottle will produce a stationary wave
49.	D	A thermistor's resistance varies inversely as the temperature change
50.	B	Total momentum before = Total momentum after 0 = $m_1 v_1 + m_2 v_2$ -1000 (V_r) = 10(150) V_r = -1.5 m/s So recoil (backward) velocity is 1.5 m/s

Question	Answer	Explanation
51.	B	Maximum height means that $v = 0$ m/s , $u = 16$ m/s, $a = 10$ m/s^2 , $s = ?$ We use $v^2 = u^2 - 2\,a\,s$ $\qquad 0^2 = 16^2 - 2\,(10)\,s$ $\qquad s = 12.8$ m
52.	C	Angular velocity $\rightarrow$ $\omega = 2\pi f = 2\pi\,(50/60) = 5.23$ rad/s
53.	E	We know that $I = \dfrac{k}{D^2}$ So we use $I_1 D_1^2 = I_2 D_2^2 \rightarrow I_1 (5)^2 = I_2 (10)^2$ $\qquad\qquad\qquad I_1 : I_2 = 100 : 25$ $\qquad\qquad\qquad I_1 : I_2 = 4 : 1$
54.	E	Highest energy means highest frequency, of the listed choices 'X-rays' would be the only EM with the highest frequency
55.	D	$\Delta KE = KE_f - KE_i = 1/2\,(1000)(-10)^2 - 1/2\,(1000)(25)^2$ $\Delta KE = -262500$ J or decreased by 262.5 kJ
56.	D	As the ball fall its speed and velocity would increase, also as the air resistance or drag force. The only thing that remains the same would be 'acceleration due to gravity' which is always about 10 m/s^2 throughout the entire fall.
57.	B	In double slit experiment we must remember that wavelength is directly proportional to number of fringes. So to increase number of fringes we must increase the wavelength (Wavelength is inversely proportional to frequency) or decrease the frequency
58.	B	We use $\qquad\qquad s = ut + 1/2\,a\,t^2$ $\qquad\qquad\qquad 500 = 0(t) + 1/2\,(10)\,t^2$ $\qquad\qquad\qquad t = 10$ seconds
59.	A	Horizontal distance travelled we can ignore acceleration here $\qquad$ Horizontal Distance = Horizontal speed x time $\qquad\qquad\qquad = 30$ x 10 $\qquad\qquad\qquad = 300$ meter
60.	D	We konw that at T = 2 seconds $V_x = 30$ m/s and $V_y = 20$ m/s So $V^2 = V_x^2 + V_y^2 \rightarrow V = 36$ m/s

Question	Answer	Explanation
61.	C	Greatest or maximum destructive interference occurs when two waves are out of phase or phase difference is 180°
62.	A	Greatest momentum under the condition of same velocity means that the mass must be greatest. In this case the heaviest of all would be alpha particles, consist of helium nucleus
63.	D	Beat is created when two or more sound are produced with a difference frequency or pitch.
64.	B	We use $v = f\lambda$ → Electromagnetic wave has a speed of 3×10^8 m/s $3 \times 10^8 = (6 \times 10^9) \times \lambda$ $\lambda = 5$ cm
65.	E	Total resistance we break them into R_{t1}, R_{t2} and R_{t3}, assuming that all resistor has a resistance of R. $1/R_{t1} = 1/R + 1/R + 1/R$ → $R_{t1} = R/3$ $1/R_{t2} = 1/R + 1/R$ → $R_{t2} = R/2$ $R_{t3} = R$ Now we look at R_{t1}, R_{t2} and R_{t3} connected in series so we find the sum $R_{total} = R_{t1} + R_{t2} + R_{t3}$ $66 = R/3 + R/2 + R$ $R = 36\ \Omega$
66.	C	Sound wave are polarized from the begining of creation, so even if it is passed thru a grid no polarization is taking place any further
67.	A	Density is inversely proportional to volume, as water cools its volume decreases so the density would increase
68.	A	Alpha particle is composed of helium nucleus, which contains only 2 protons and 2 neutrons.
69.	A	To find current we use $I = Q / t$ $I = 300 / (60)$ $I = 5$ A
70.	B	Evaporation differs from boiling in a sense that it does not necessary occurs at boiling point, it can occur at any temperature as long as liquid molecules have enough energy to change its phase.

Question	Answer	Explanation
71.	A	Alpha has the lowest penetration ability, it can be blocked by a piece of cloth or paper easily
72.	D	According to Einstein light has (nearly) no mass so it will not experience any gravitational effect
73.	D	If we increase intensity of light the number of emitted photo-electrons will also increase
74.	C	We need to find E_{total} $E_{total} = E_{kinetic} + $ work function $E_{total} = (3.43 + 3.2) \times 10^{-19}$ $E_{total} = 6.63 \times 10^{-19}$ J $hf = 6.63 \times 10^{-19}$ $f = (6.63 \times 10^{-19}) / (6.63 \times 10^{-34})$ $f = 1 \times 10^{15}$ Hz
75.	C	To find velocity we use $E_{kinetic} = 1/2\, m_{electron} \times v^2_{electron}$ $v^2 = 2 \times (3.43 \times 10^{-19}) \times (9.1 \times 10^{-31})$ $v = 8.68 \times 10^5$ m/s

Score Range

Raw Score	Conversion
64 - 75	800
58 - 63	750 - 790
53 - 57	720 - 740
48 - 52	690 - 710
42 - 47	650 - 680
38 - 41	590 - 640
33 - 37	540 - 580
28 - 32	510 - 530
23 - 27	450 - 500
17 - 22	400 - 440
0 - 16	270 - 390

Raw Score   =   Correct Answers   -   0.25 Wrong Answers

$$\boxed{} = \boxed{} - 0.25 \times \boxed{}$$

Question 1-3 use the following information

Velocity (m/s)

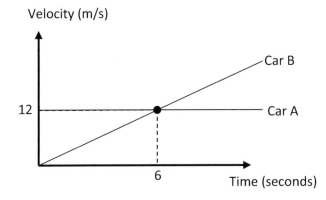

1. At what time will car B catch up with car A ?

a)   3   seconds

b)   6   seconds

c)   12   seconds

d)   18   seconds

e)   20   seconds

2.   How far have car B travel the instant car A catches up with it ?

a)   60   m

b)   72   m

c)   108   m

d)   144   m

e)   180   m

3. The instant car B catches up with car A , car B starts to decelerate and comes to rest within 3 seconds, what is the deceleration of car B ?

a)   2   m/s^2

b)   4   m/s^2

c)   6   m/s^2

d)   8   m/s^2

e)   10   m/s^2

Question 4 - 8 use the following information

a) Conservation of linear momentum

b) Conservation of angular momentum

c) Law of conservation of energy

d) Conservation of momentum and kinetic energy

e) Newton's law of gravitational

Match the law to the ideas below:

4. A planet orbits the Sun at greater velocity when it is closer to the Sun

5. A car hits a stationary truck, calculate velocity of the truck if the car comes to rest

6. A planet orbits the Sun but is not pull towards it

7. A ball bouncing on the frictionless floor

8. An atomic collision

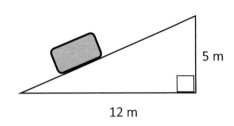

5 m

12 m

A 5 kilogram box is at rest on an incline plane

9. What is the frictional force acting on the box?

a)   18.3   N

b)   19.2   N

c)   22.4   N

d)   28.3   N

e)   31.5   N

10. If we need to push the box up with the acceleration of 2 m/s^2 , what is minimum force needed ?

a)   18.3   N

b)   26.7   N

c)   38.5   N

d)   42.5   N

e)   48.5   N

11. How much work is done against friction in order to push the box up ?

a)   250   N

b)   180   N

c)   150   N

d)   120   N

e)   80   N

12. A copper wire of length 5 m has a resistance of 6 Ω. What is the resistance of this wire if it has the length of 10 Km ?

a)   10   Ω

b)   12   Ω

c)   18   Ω

d)   10   k Ω

e)   12   k Ω

13. A meter wire has a current of 4 mA applied , it experienced a force of 10 N. What is the magnetic field on the wire ?

a)   2500   T

b)   400   T

c)   250   T

d)   40   T

e)   25   T

Question 14 - 16 use the following information

A step-down transformer has an a.c. input voltage of 5,000 volt with a winding of 4,000 turns. The output side has a winding of 100 turns, with a 100% efficiency.

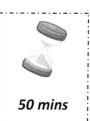

14. Which of the following is true ?

a) Current input = Current output

b) Voltage input = Voltage output

c) Power input = Power output

d) Voltage input < Voltage output

e) Current input > Current output

15. If the input current is 0.2 A, what is the output current ?

a)   0   A

b)   0.005   A

c)   0.05   A

d)   0.8   A

e)   8   A

16. If the input voltage is change to d.c. voltage of 2500 volt ,what is the output voltage ?

a)   100,000 V

b)   10,000 V

c)   1,000   V

d)   10   V

e)   0   V

17. How does heat energy from the Sun travels to the Earth ?

a)   Conduction

b)   Convection

c)   Radiation

d)   Emission

e)   Polarization

18. Which of the following is not part of second law of thermodynamic ?

a)   total energy in the system is conserved

b)   heat cannot flow from hot to cold

c)   entropy of the system is increasing

d)   entropy remain constant at equilibrium

e)   external energy can cause heat flow from cold to hot

SAT Physics Practice-Test

19. An PHEV (plug-in hybrid electric vehicle) has a motor of 80 W, the car and the passenger have a combined mass of 2000 kg. If the car is fully charged it can travel at the average speed of 15 m/s for an hour. What is the efficiency of this system ?

a)   100 %

b)   88 %

c)   78 %

d)   65 %

e)   55 %

20. Which of the following is true about 'entropy' ?

a)   is decreasing

b)   is increasing

c)   can be predicted

d)   is constant

e)   cannot be calculated

21. What happens to the intensity of sound if the amplitude of sound is doubled and the distance of the source is tripled ?

a)   increased by 9 /2

b)   increased by 3 /2

c)   decreased by 2 / 9

d)   decreased by 2 /3

e)   no change

22. A bat emits a sonar at the speed of 340 m/s to its cave 2 Km far away, given that the bat is moving with the speed of 5 m/s. How long will it take the pulse to travel back to the bat ?

a)   less than 5.9 seconds

b)   more than 5.9 seconds

c)   exactly 11.8 seconds

d)   less than 11.8 seconds

e)   exactly 13.2 seconds

23. Which of the following electromagnetic wave have the lowest frequency ?

a)   Radio wave

b)   Ultraviolet

c)   Visible light

d)   Sound

e)   Gamma ray

24. Which of the following must be true about anti-proton ?

a)   positively charged

b)   same mass as neutron

c)   same charge as electron

d)   same mass as photon

e)   has no charge and no mass

25. Which of the following is TRUE about Rutherford atomic model ?

a)   atoms are not empty space

b)   most mass are not at the nucleus

c)   electron are at the nucleus

d)   atoms are positively charged

e)   nucleus are positively charged

26. When electromagnetic wave strikes a metal photo-electron is emitted out. If the intensity of light of increase then

a)   number of emitted electrons increase

b)   speed of electrons increase

c)   speed of light decreases

d)   number of emitted protons increase

e)   speed of protons increase

27. A ball of mass 2 kg rolls 4 meter on a floor at the speed of 12 m/s comes to rest due to frictional force. How much frictional force is experienced by the ball ?

a)   36   N

b)   32   N

c)   20   N

d)   18   N

e)   8   N

28. What is the average velocity of the car moving in circular track with a radius of 5 meter in 3 minutes ?

a) $\pi / 18$ ms^{-1}

b) $5\pi / 18$ ms^{-1}

c) $\pi / 3$ ms^{-1}

d) $5\pi / 3$ ms^{-1}

e)   0   ms^{-1}

29. How much energy is required to push 5 kg box horizontally to a constant speed of 20 m/s ?

a)   100   N

b)   500   N

c)   800   N

d)   1000   N

e)   2000   N

SAT Physics Practice-Test

30. Which form of energy is not related to the Sun's energy?

a)   solar

b)   nuclear

c)   wind-mill

d)   hydro-electric

e)   biomass

31. A uniform one meter long beam rest on two supports equally spaced from both end. Which of the following is TRUE about the diagram below ?

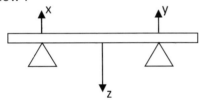

a) there is a resultant moment

b) there is a resultant force

c) total upward force equal twice total downward force

d) the resultant force equal zero but not the resultant moment

e) the two upward force are equal to each other

32. How much work is done in moving a charge of 2 coulomb from a low potential difference of -4 volt to a high potential difference of 4 volt ?

a)   -8   J

b)   -16   J

c)   0   J

d)   8   J

e)   16   J

33. A charge of 10 C and -10 C is placed 2 meter apart, how much electric force is experienced by the charges ?

a)   900   GN

b)   450   GN

c)   225   GN

d)   -450   GN

e)   -225   GN

34. If the distance between the charges is halved, which of the following will happen to the electric force between the charges ?

a)   quadrupled

b)   doubled

c)   stay the same

d)   reduce by half

e)   reduce by quarter

35. A charge of -1 C is placed in the electric field of 5 N/C, how much work must be done to move the charge 10 cm away from the field ?

a)   0   J

b)   0.5   J

c)   1   J

d)   5   J

e)   10   J

36. Which of the following explains the phenomenon of spectrum produced when white light falls on to a diffraction grating ?

a) refraction

b) reflection

c) interference

d) polarization

e) coherence

37. Which of the following is true about a sound of siren of an ambulance heard by a person sleeping in the house as the ambulance move away from the house ?

a)   pitch of the siren increases

b)   pitch of the siren decreases

c)   pitch of the siren remain constant

d)   quality of wave increases

e)   quality of wave decreases

38. In 'isochoric' which of the following property must remain constant ?

a)   Pressure

b)   Volume

c)   Temperature

d)   Mass

e)   Energy

39. A can has a volume of 400 cm^3 and the pressure of the compressed gas inside is five times atmospheric pressure. How much volume would the gas occupied if it was released into the air ?

a)   2000 cm^3

b)   1000 cm^3

c)   500 cm^3

d)   100 cm^3

e)   80 cm^3

40. Difference between lower fixed point and upper fixed point of a thermometer is

a)   0   k

b)   100 k

c)   150 k

d)   273 k

e)   373 k

SAT Physics Practice-Test

41. If one-volt is applied to an electron, how much energy will it have ?

a) 9.11×10^{-31} J

b) 8.31×10^{-27} J

c) 6.63×10^{-24} J

d) 3.0×10^{-21} J

e) 1.6×10^{-19} J

42. Which particles are emitted off during beta decay ?

a)   atoms

b)   neutrons

c)   protons

d)   electrons

e)   nucleons

43. How much energy is delivered on a metal if an electromagnetic wave of frequency 10^{17} Hz falls on the metal ?

a) 6.63×10^{-51} J

b) 6.63×10^{-34} J

c) 6.63×10^{-17} J

d) 6.63×10^{-2} J

e) 6.63×10^{2} J

44. A barometer is used to measure

a) current in wire

b) pressure of air

c) temperature of the liquid

d) volume of a gas

e) density of a liquid

45. Which of the following is measured in Newton ?

a) momentum x distance

b) energy / time

c) mass x velocity

d) energy / distance

e) momentum x acceleration

46. A copper wire with a diameter of 1mm can with stand a pressure of 10^{9} Pascal. What is the maximum force applied to this wire ?

a)   1.57   GN

b)   3.14   MN

c)   7.96   kN

d)   0.785   kN

e)   314   N

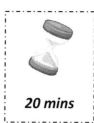

47. What is the minimum force required to topple a 2 kilogram cuboid of volume one meter cube to another face?

a)   5   N

b)   10   N

c)   20   N

d)   40   N

e)   60   N

48. A ten gram base-ball with an initial kinetic energy of 5 joules rise up vertically to a maximum height of how many meter ?

a)   5   m

b)   10   m

c)   50   m

d)   100   m

e)   250   m

49. Which of the following statement must be TRUE concerning a car through a circular track ?

a)   it is moving with a constant speed

b)   there is no gravitational force acting

c)   there is no acceleration

d)   there is no frictional force

e)   its speed is increasing

50. Which of the following process does not require heat supply ?

a)   freezing

b)   melting

c)   boiling

d)   evaporation

e)   sublimation

51. The sum of all microscopic potential and kinetic energy of the molecules in an object is known as

a)   gravitational energy

b)   atomic energy

c)   chemical energy

d)   nuclear energy

e)   internal energy

Question 52 - 54 use the following information

The resistance of the resistor in the circuit are all identical. The total resistance of the circuit is 15 kΩ.

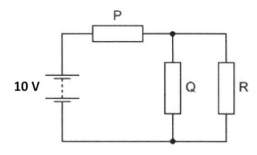

54. What is the amount of energy dissipated at P in one minute ?

a)   0.27   J

b)   0.5   J

c)   3   J

d)   5   J

e)   27   J

52. What is the value of the resistance of resistor P?

a)   10   Ω

b)   20   Ω

c)   10   kΩ

d)   20   kΩ

e)   45   kΩ

55. Five picometer is equivalent to

a)   0.0000000000005 m

b)   0.000000000005 m

c)   0.00000000005 m

d)   0.0000000005 m

e)   0.00000005 m

53. What is the current through resistor R ?

a)   1/3   mA

b)   2/3   mA

c)   1   mA

d)   4/3   mA

e)   5/3   mA

56. A five centimeter spring is hung with a load of four Newton , it extends 'x' centimeter. What is the length of the spring (in cm) if the load is tripled ?

a)   x/3

b)   x

c)   3x

d)   5 + x/3

e)   5 + 3x

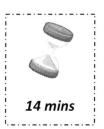

57. An object of 3 kg moving with the speed of 4 m/s strikes a wall and bounces back horizontally with a sound produced. Which of the following statement is TRUE ?

a) total kinetic energy after collision is 24 joules

b) total kinetic energy after collision is less than 24 joules

c) total kinetic energy before collision is more than 24 joules

d) total kinetic energy before collision is less than 24 joules

e) total kinetic energy before and after collision is 24 joules

Question 58 - 60 use the following information

An object is placed 6 centimeters from the convex lens, that has a focal length of 4 centimeters. An image is produced after the light is turned on.

58. How far is the image from the object ?

a)   6   cm

b)   10   cm

c)   12   cm

d)   16   cm

e)   18   cm

59. Which of the following is/are the property of the image produced ?

a)   Diminished

b)   Diminished and Inverted

c)   Laterally Inverted

d)   Virtual image

e)   Real image

60. What is the magnification size of the image?

a)   0.5

b)   1

c)   1.5

d)   2

e)   2.5

61. If an object is placed behind the focus of a concave lens then the image produced by a concave lens will always be

a)   real

b)   virtual

c)   inverted

d)   magnified

e)   virtual and magnified

62. When one vibrating tuning fork causes another tuning fork to vibrates at the same frequency, it is said that both are

a)   amplitude

b)   loudness

c)   resonated

d)   polarized

e)   amplified

Question 63 - 65 use the following information

A 150 g ball is fired from a spring toy cannon, whose mass is 1kg, that was compressed by 'x' meter. The recoil velocity of the cannon is 3 m/s.

63. What is the velocity of the ball ?

a)   4.5   m/s

b)   6   m/s

c)   9   m/s

d)   15   m/s

e)   20   m/s

10 mins

64. What was the elastic potential of the spring in the toy cannon ?

a)   17.3   J

b)   34.5   J

c)   69   J

d)   83.2   J

e)   111.3   J

65. What is the impulse experienced by the toy gun?

a)   1.5   kg m/s

b)   2.5   kg m/s

c)   3.0   kg m/s

d)   4.5   kg m/s

e)   6.0   kg m/s

SAT Physics Practice-Test

66. Moon has one-sixth the acceleration due to gravity of the Earth. If an object that weight 240 N on Earth is brought to the Moon how much will it weight ?

a)   24   N

b)   40   N

c)   60   N

d)   240   N

e)   1440   N

67. The relationship between pitch and loudness is

a)   directly proportional

b)   linearly proportional with y-intercept

c)   inversely proportional

d)   inversely proportional with y-intercept

e)   not directly or inversely proportional

68. Which of the following illustrates the property of a super conductor ?

a)   high resistivity

b)   highly volatile

c)   flammable

d)   low energy loss

e)   low voltage

69. A charge of 20 coulomb passes through a wire with a resistance of 3 Ω in one minute. How much work is done by the charges ?

a)   20   J

b)   15   J

c)   10   J

d)   5   J

e)   1   J

70. Light signals travel in fiber optics from one end to another end due to which of the following event ?

a)   total internal refraction

b)   total internal reflection

c)   total external diffraction

d)   photo-electric effect

e)   polarization

71. Which of the following particle is positively charged and lightest ?

a)   positron

b)   proton

c)   electron

d)   nucleus

e)   neutron

72. An object falls with the speed of 16 m/s, at this point the weight and the air resistance are equal. What will be its speed after 2 seconds ?

a)   0   m/s

b)   16   m/s

c)   26   m/s

d)   32   m/s

e)   36   m/s

73. Which particle can move at the speed of light ?

a)   positron

b)   proton

c)   photon

d)   electron

e)   none of the above

74. A charge of 5 C move with a velocity of 10 m/s parallel to the magnetic field of 25 T. How much force is experienced by the charge ?

a)   2500   N

b)   1250   N

c)   625   N

d)   125   N

e)   0   N

75. A wire is folded into a square shape of length 2 m pass through a magnetic field of 3.5T in 0.5 seconds. How much e.m.f. is induced on the wire ?

a)   42   V

b)   28   V

c)   14   V

d)   7   V

e)   3.5   V

Answer Key 3

Question	Answer	Explanation
1.	C	Distant of Car A = Distant of Car B $\rightarrow$ s = ut + 1/2 at^2 $\qquad S_A \qquad = \qquad S_B$ $\qquad V_A \times T \qquad = U_B T + 1/2\, a\, T^2 \rightarrow$ a = slope of car B = 12/6 = 2 m/s^2 $\qquad 12\, T \qquad = (0)\, T + 1/2\, (2)\, T^2$ $\qquad\quad T \qquad = 12$ seconds
2.	D	$S_B = S_A = V_A \times T = 12 \times 12 = 144$ m
3.	D	At t = 12 seconds $\rightarrow$ speed of car B is 24 m/s (by using V- U = at) To slow down we use a = (v - u) / t $\qquad\qquad\qquad\qquad$ a = (0 - 24) / 3 $\qquad\qquad\qquad\qquad$ a = - 8 m/s^2
4.	B	The law of conservation of angular momentum $\rightarrow$ L = m v r If 'r' radius decreases then 'v' orbital velocity should increase.
5.	A	The law of conservation of linear momentum says Total momentum before collision = Total momentum after collision
6.	E	According to Newton's law of gravitational Two bodies will exerts a force towards each other and these gravitational force must be equal
7.	C	A ball bouncing on a frictionless floor will not lose its energy so we can say that it's total energy is conserved
8.	D	In an atomic collision momentum and kinetic energy are always conserved
9.	B	 $f = mg\cos\theta$ $f = 50 \times (adj / hyp)$ $f = 50 \times (5 /13)$ $f = 19.2$ N

Question	Answer	Explanation
10.	E	 $F_{net} = F - f - mg\cos\theta$ $ma = F - f - mg\cos\theta$ $(5)(2) = F - 19.2 - 19.2$ $F = 48.5$ N
11.	A	$W_f = f \times d_{incline} = 19.2 \times 13 = 250$ N
12.	E	$R_1 / L_1 = R_2 / L_2$ $6 / 5 = R_2 / 10k$ $R_2 = 12$ kΩ
13.	A	$F = B I L$ $10 = B(4 \times 10^{-3})(1)$ $B = 2500$ Tesla
14.	C	In a transformer Power input is always equal to Power output (given that the efficiency is 100 %)
15.	E	$I_{in} \times N_{in} = I_{out} \times N_{out}$ $0.2 \times 4000 = I_{out} \times 100$ $I_{out} = 8$ A
16.	E	0 Volt Because transformer only works with an A.C. input not D.C.
17.	C	Energy from the Sun travels to the Earth in form of 'electromagnetic waves' these wave are 'radiated' from the Sun
18.	A	Total energy in the system is conserved was part of the First law of thermodynamic

Question	Answer	Explanation
19.	C	% efficiency = Power output / Power input x 100% $\quad$ = [(1/2 m v^2) / time] / 80 $\quad$ x 100% $\quad$ = [1/2 x 2000 x 15^2 / 3600] /80 x 100% $\quad$ = 78 %
20.	B	Entropy is always increasing (until equilibrium point)
21.	C	$I_1 d_1^2 / A_1$ $\quad$ = $I_2 d_2^2 / A_2$ $\rightarrow$ where I is intensity, A is amplitude and d is distance $I_1 (1)^2 / (1)$ = $I_2 (3)^2/(2)$ I_2 = 2/9 I_1
22.	D	We first look at the time travel by the sound Time = distance back and forth / speed Time = (4000 meter) / 340 Time = 11. 8 seconds for sound to come back , if the bat was stationary But the bat was moving forward as well so the time take will be lesser than 11.8 seconds
23.	A	Radio wave has the least energy of all so it will have the lowest frequency
24.	C	Anti-proton has exactly the same mass as proton but the opposite charge Which means anti-proton has a negative charge similar charge to electron
25.	E	Nucleus contain protons , hence the charge of the nucleus will be positive
26.	A	When the intensity increases the number of emitted will also increase
27.	A	$\quad$ $v^2 = u^2 - 2as$ $\rightarrow 0^2 = 12^2 - 2$ a (4) $\rightarrow$ a = 18 m/s^2 $\quad\quad$ $f = F$ $\quad\quad$ $f = m a$ $\quad\quad$ $f = 2 (18) = 36$ N
28.	E	Average velocity = change in displacement / change in time $\quad\quad$ = 0 m / 180 s $\quad\quad$ = 0 ms^{-1}
29.	D	Work = change in energy KE = 1/2 m v^2 KE = 1/2 (5) (20^2) KE = 1000 N
30.	B	All of the choices is a product of Sun's energy except for nuclear

Question	Answer	Explanation
31.	E	As the beam is uniform and the support are equally spaced from both end, we can conclude that Force at Z = Force at X + Force at Y And force at X and at Y must also be equal since they are equally spaced from both end points
32.	D	Work = q x Δv = 2 (4 - (-4)) = 2 (8) = 16 J
33.	E	F = k q_1 q_2 / r^2 = (9 x 10^9) (10) (-10) / (2^2) F = -225 GN
34.	A	F is inversely proportional to R^2 So if R decrease by half so F will increase by four times or quadrupled $F_1 R_1^2 = F_2 R_2^2$ $(F_1)(1)^2 = F_2 (0.5)$ $F_2 = 4F_1$
35.	B	W = q E D W = (1)(5)(0.1) W = 0.5 J
36.	C	When white light falls on diffraction grating we can observed a pattern of fringes of spectrum of colors on the screen or we can say they interfere with one another
37.	B	According to Doppler effect as the source of sound move closer to the observer the pitch or the frequency would increases from the original frequency
38.	B	In 'isochoric' the volume will not change
39.	A	<u>Can</u> <u>Air</u> $P_1 V_1$ = $P_2 V_2$ 5(400) = 1(V) V = 2000 cm^3
40.	B	Difference between upper fixed point (100°c) and lower fixed point (0°c) is 100 degree Celsius or we can say it is equal to 100K
41.	E	1 eV = 1.6 x 10^{-19} J
42.	D	During a beta decay an electron will be emitted off
43.	C	E = hf E = (6.63 x 10^{-34} x 10^{17}) = 6.63 x 10^{-17} J
44.	B	A barometer is used to measure atmospheric pressure , or pressure of air

Question	Answer	Explanation
45.	D	We know that Newton is a unit of Force, so Work = change in energy Force x distance = energy Force = energy / distance
46.	D	Pressure = force / area Force = Pressure x area Force = 10^9 x π x $(0.005)^2$ Force = 785 N or 0.785 k N
47.	B	If the volume is one meter cube we can say each side has a length of 1 meter Total ccw moment = Total cw moment 20 x 0.5 = F x 1 F = 10 N
48.	C	According to law of conservation of energy KE = PE 5 = m g h 5 = (0.01) (10) h h = 50 meter
49.	A	A car moving in circular track would experienced a centripetal force which will cause it to move in circular motion with a constant speed but not constant velocity
50.	A	An substance that freezes does not require any input heat, instead it will release energy out to the surrounding
51.	E	Internal energy is the sum of all microscopic potential and kinetic energy of the molecules in an object
52.	C	The total resistance = $R_P + R_{QR}$ 15 kΩ = R + R/2 R = 10 kΩ
53.	A	V_{Total} = I x R_{total} → 10 = I (15 k) → I_{total} = 2/3 mA Since R_Q and R_R are equal so the current from I total will divide itself equally We can say current in resistor R is 1/3 mA

Question	Answer	Explanation
54.	A	Heat $= I^2 R \times t = (2/3 \times 10^{-3})^2 \times (10 \times 10^3) \times (1 \times 60)$ Heat $= 0.27$ J
55.	B	5 pm $= 5 \times 10^{-12} = 0.000000000005$ m
56.	E	If the load is tripled the extension is also tripled So we can say extension is 3x cm Total length = 5 + 3x cm
57.	B	The object has initial KE $= 1/2 (3) (4^2) = 24$ Joules Once it strikes the wall sound is produced to total energy after collision will be less than 24 joules
58.	E	$1/f = 1/d_i + 1/d_o$ $1/4 = 1/d_i + 1/6$ $d_i = 12$ cm distance is from the object is 6 + 12 = 18 cm
59.	E	The image produced by the lens is on the opposite site of the object, which is considered to be real image (inverted and magnified as well)
60.	D	$M = d_i / d_o = 12 / 6 = 2$
61.	B	The image produced by concave lens will show a virtual image(and diminished) if object was behind the focus.
62.	C	If one fork causes another to vibrate at the same frequency we say resonance occur or they resonated
63.	E	$P_i = P_f$ $(0.15)(v) = (1)(3)$ $V = 20$ m/s
64.	B	Total energy from spring = total KE of the ball and canon Ball Canon $1/2(0.15)(20^2) + 1/2(1)(3^2) = 34.5$ Joules
65.	C	$\Delta P = m \times \Delta v$ $\Delta P = 1(-3-0)$ $\Delta P = -3$ kg m/s or 3 kg m/s backward

Question	Answer	Explanation
66.	B	$W_{Moon} = W_{Earth}/6$ $W_{Moon} = 240/6$ $W_{Moon} = 40$ N
67.	E	Pitch and loudness are not related to each other
68.	D	Super conductors allow electrons to flow pass easily without any heat loss or lost in energy taking place
69.	A	$V = I R \rightarrow V = (q/t) \times R \rightarrow V = (20/60) \times 3 \rightarrow V = 1$ volt Work $= q V = 20 \times 1 = 20$ Joules
70.	B	Total internal reflection allows light to be reflected internally in the fiber optics from one end to another end
71.	A	Positron is positively charge and has the same mass as electron (lightest)
72.	B	The object is said to have reached the terminal velocity, which means it will fall at the constant velocity until it hit the ground
73.	C	Photons are massless, according to Einstein they vibrate carrying energy from the Sun
74.	E	When the charge move parallel to the field no force is induced, so 0 N
75.	B	e.m.f. $= \dfrac{\Phi}{\Delta t} = \dfrac{B\,(Area)}{\Delta t} = \dfrac{3.5 \times (2 \times 2)}{0.5} = 28$ V

Score Range

Raw Score	Conversion
65 - 75	800
59 - 64	750 - 790
53 - 58	720 - 740
48 - 52	690 - 710
42 - 47	650 - 680
36 - 41	590 - 640
30 - 35	540 - 580
25 - 29	510 - 530
20 - 24	450 - 500
15 - 19	400 - 440
0 - 15	270 - 390

Raw Score   =   Correct Answers   -   0.25 Wrong Answers

$$\boxed{} = \boxed{} - 0.25 \times \boxed{}$$

Practice Test 4

Question 1 - 5 use the following graphs

a)

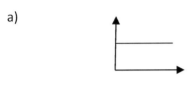

b)

c)

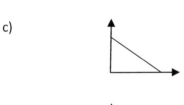

d)

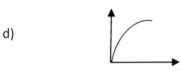

e)

1. Speed vs Time graph of a ball rolling down a rough incline plane

2. Displacement vs Time graph of a rocket moving down with a constant acceleration

3. Acceleration vs Time graph of a bottle dropped on the Moon

4. Gravitational Potential Energy vs Time graph of a paratrooper jumping from the plane

5. Kinetic Energy vs Velocity of a rocket leaving the Earth

Question 6 - 8 use the following information

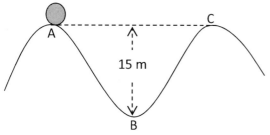

15 m

A ball of mass 5 kg rolls down the hill from the height of 15 meter. Ignoring friction and air-resistance.

6. What is the velocity of the ball at the bottom of the hills ?

a)   6.1   m/s

b)   8.6   m/s

c)   12.2   m/s

d)   17.3   m/s

e)   21.2   m/s

8. What is the total change in gravitational potential energy as the ball move from A to C ?

a)   0   J

b)   375   J

c)   750   J

d)   1125   J

e)   1500   J

7. Which of the following will be TRUE about the ball rolling down if there is friction ?

a) the ball will still reached point C

b) the ball will go over point C at first roll

c) the ball will stop immediately at point B

d) the ball will not reach point C and roll back

e) the ball will not reach point B immediately

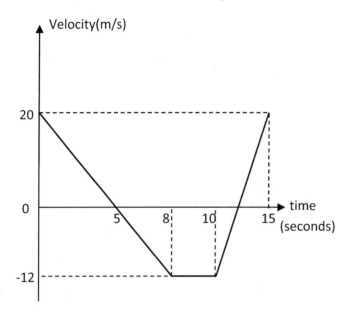

The graph above show the velocity versus time graph of a bus travelling in town, with a total displacement of twenty-eight meter.

9. What is the displacement during first eight second of the journey ?

a)   18   m

b)   32   m

c)   44   m

d)   50   m

e)   68   m

10. What is the average speed of the bus during first eight seconds of the journey ?

a)   3   m/s

b)   4   m/s

c)   6   m/s

d)   8.5   m/s

e)   10.5   m/s

11. What is the acceleration of the bus during last five seconds ?

a)   8.6   m/s^2

b)   7.2   m/s^2

c)   6.4   m/s^2

d)   5.2   m/s^2

e)   4.3   m/s^2

12. What is the average velocity of the bus during the whole fifteen seconds journey ?

a)   1.9   m/s

b)   3.5   m/s

c)   6.9   m/s

d)   9.8   m/s

e)   11.5   m/s

Question 13 - 17 use the following information

a) Diode

b) Thermistor

c) Ideal resistor

d) Filament lamp

e) LDR

13. Current is directly proportional to voltage

14. Resistance decreases as the temperature increases

15. Allows current to flow pass if a voltage applied is more than 0.7 volt

16. Produces heat as more current pass through

17. Resistance increases as the brightness increases

18. A battery with e.m.f. of 20 V is connected with a bulb of 8Ω resistance, given that the internal resistance of the cell is 2Ω. How much power is dissipated by the bulb ?

a)   8   W

b)   16   W

c)   32   W

d)   40   W

e)   60   W

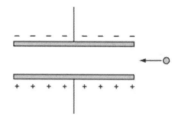

19. A charge enters a region of electric field. Which of the following is true ?

	Vertical component	Horizontal component
a)	Constant acceleration	Constant acceleration
b)	Constant acceleration	Constant velocity
c)	Constant velocity	Constant velocity
d)	Constant velocity	Constant acceleration
e)	Constant force	Constant acceleration

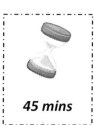

45 mins

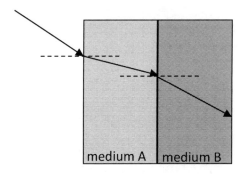

medium A   medium B

Medium A has a refractive index of 1.43

Medium B has a refractive index of 1.25

20. If the light enters medium A at the angle of 43°, then what is the angle of refraction ?

a)   23.4

b)   28.5

c)   31.2

d)   33.1

e)   37.2

21. What is the speed of light in medium B ?

a) 3.8×10^8 m/s

b) 3.0×10^8 m/s

c) 2.6×10^8 m/s

d) 2.4×10^8 m/s

e) 2.1×10^8 m/s

22. Which of the following is true ?

(I) angle that light enter the glass at A and emerging out at B is same

(II) speed of light in A is greater than in B

(III) medium A is less dense than medium B

a)   (I) only

b)   (I) and (II) only

c)   (III) only

d)   (II) and (III) only

e)   none of them

23. A person standing 7 m from a flat mirror see his image, which of the following is/are true about the image produced ?

(I) Real

(II) Magnified

(III) Inverted

a)   (I) only

b)   (I) and (II) only

c)   (III) only

d)   (II) and (III) only

e)   none of them

24. Which of the following is true about image produced by a pin-hole camera ?

a)   Image is virtual

b)   Image is always same size as object

c)   Image is laterally inverted

d)   Focus is at the hole

e)   Focus is at the image

25. Which of the following wave cannot be polarized ?

a)   Radio wave

b)   Ultraviolet

c)   Visible light

d)   Sound

e)   Gamma ray

26. A concrete slab with length of 45 cm has a coefficient of linear expansion of 12×10^{-6} /°C. If it was heated from the temperature of 15°C to 65°C then what is the increase in length?

a)   0.0027 cm

b)   0.027   cm

c)   0.27   cm

d)   1.35   cm

e)   2.7   cm

27. If the density of a liquid mercury is five times more than the density of a solid aluminum at room temperature, then which of the following is true ?

a) Atoms of mercury have greater mass than aluminum

b) Atoms of aluminum has greater mass than mercury

c) Atoms of mercury move faster than mercury

d) Atoms of aluminum move faster than mercury

e) Atoms in form of liquid take up less space than atom of solid

28. An isolated system gives off 3000 joules of heat, while the internal energy of the system is decreased by 6500 joules. How much work was done by the system ?

a)   9500   J

b)   8500   J

c)   6000   J

d)   3500   J

e)   2500   J

Question 29 - 31 use the following information

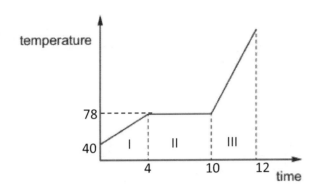

The graph above shows the change in temperature of liquid ethanol during the time it was heated by an electric heater of 2.5 kW.

29. Which of the following is true about the phase II ?

a)   Ethanol is freezing

b)   Ethanol is melting

c)   Ethanol is giving of heat

d)   Ethanol is burning

e)   Ethanol is boiling

30. How much energy was required to completely evaporate this ethanol ?

a)   900   J

b)   1500   J

c)   900   kJ

d)   1500   kJ

e)   2400   kJ

31. Which of the following is true about phase I and phase II ?

a)   no change in temperature occur

b)   both are in same state

c)   heat is released to the surrounding

d)   the liquid is expanding

e)   heat is supplied to the ethanol

32. How much energy is needed approximately to heat 600g of water at 30 °C to 60°C ? (specific heat capacity of water is 4,200 J/kg °C

a)   76500 J

b)   75600 J

c)   65700 J

d)   57600 J

e)   56070 J

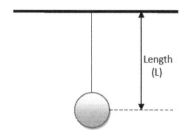

A pendulum of length 10 cm is swinging freely, without air resistance. A bob has a mass of 200g and the weight of the string can be ignored.

35. What is the centripetal force on the pendulum ?

a)   0.4   N

b)   0.8   N

c)   1.2   N

d)   4   N

e)   8   N

33. How long does it take the pendulum to move from top left to top right ?

a)   0.628   s

b)   0.428   s

c)   0.314   s

d)   0.216   s

e)   0.157   s

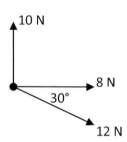

36. What is the vertical component of resultant force ?

a)   2.1   N

b)   4.0   N

c)   6.2   N

d)   13.1   N

e)   18.4   N

34. What is the angular velocity of this pendulum ?

a)   2   m/s

b)   3.1   m/s

c)   4   m/s

d)   6.2   m/s

e)   7.1   m/s

37. A girl walk 4 meter north and 6 meter west, then she walked 2 meter north. What is the straight line distance from the starting point to the ending point ?

a)   6   m

b) $6\sqrt{2}$ m

c)   10   m

d) $10\sqrt{2}$ m

e)   12   m

38. A uniform bar of mass 20 kilogram lying on the ground is lifted from the one end. If the bar is 3 meter long, what is the minimum force required to lift it from the end ?

a)   50   N

b)   100   N

c)   150   N

d)   300   N

e)   600   N

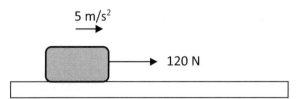

5 m/s²

120 N

39. A 4 kg box is accelerated with a force of 120N. What is the frictional force experienced by the box ?

a)   140   N

b)   120   N

c)   100   N

d)   80   N

e)   60   N

40. A box exploded into two masses of M_1 and M_2 with a velocity of 3v and v respectively. What is the ratio of M_1 to M_2 ?

a)   3:1

b)   3:2

c)   1:3

d)   2:3

e)   1:1

41. A distant planet has the same mass as the Earth but twice the radius. What is the ratio of the planet gravitation strength to Earth's gravitation strength ?

a)   1 : 4

b)   1 : 2

c)   2 : 3

d)   2 : 1

e)   4 : 1

42. What is the distant travel by the car that was initially at rest and was accelerated with $3 m/s^2$ for 6 second ?

a)   18   m

b)   36   m

c)   54   m

d)   72   m

e)   108   m

43. How much impulse was delivered by a 5000 kg truck moving at the speed of 25 m/s into the wall (and stop) ?

a)   62.5   kN·s

b)   125   kN·s

c)   250   kN·s

d)   375   kN·s

e)   425   kN·s

44. Which of the following describe power ?

a)   Energy x distance

b)   Energy x time

c)   Work x velocity

d)   Force x velocity

e)   Momentum x time

45. The quotient of weight over area is equivalent to ?

a)   Work

b)   Pressure

c)   Kinetic energy

d)   Momentum

e)   Density

46. Which of the following radiation has the greatest ionizing effect ?

a)   Alpha

b)   Beta

c)   Gamma

d)   X-rays

e)   UV-rays

47. A radioactive isotope have different number of

a)   proton

b)   electron

c)   photons

d)   positron

e)   neutron

48. A radioactive element has a half-life of 20 days, given that its initial mass is 320 g, what will be the mass left after 100 days ?

a)   5120   g

b)   2560   g

c)   40   g

d)   20   g

e)   10   g

Question 49- 52 use the following information

a) Proton

b) Positron

c) Electron

d) Neutron

e) Photon

Match the following to the description below

49. Is heaviest and located in the center of atom

50. High energy electromagnetic wave

51. Is lightest and have a positive charge

52. Result in emission of beta decay

Question 53 - 57 use the following information

a) Acceleration due to gravity

b) Length or distance

c) Angular momentum

d)Orbital velocity

e) Gravitational Force

53. Varies directly to the square of the period of a pendulum

54. Varies inversely to the square of the radius of a planet

55. Varies directly to the product of planet's masses

56. Varies inversely to the square root of the radius of a planet

57. Varies directly to product of the planet's mean radius and the planet's mass

58. Which of the following is true about a diode?

a)   has an operating current of 0.7 A

b)   has an operating voltage of 0.7 V

c)   has an operating power of 0.7 W

d)   has an operating resistance 0.7 Ω

e)   has an operating charge 0.7 C

59. The pitch of a sound is affected by

a)   amplitude of wave

b)   quality of wave

c)   intensity of wave

d)   frequency of wave

e)   speed of wave

Question 60 - 62 use the following information

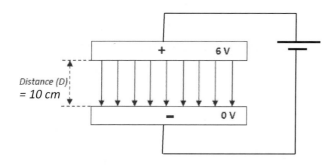

60. What is the change in electric potential if a charge move from top of the plate to middle of the parallel plate ?

a)   -6 V

b)   -3 V

c)   0 V

d)   3 V

e)   6 V

61. If a charge of 2 C is inserted between the plate of uniform electric field how much potential energy will it have ?

a)   0   J

b)   4   J

c)   6   J

d)   12   J

e)   24   J

62. If an electron is shot thru the field between the plate, which direction will it move ?

a) out of the page

b) into the page

c) curved upward

d) curved downward

e) straight through the field

63. When a monochromatic light enters the wave, what changes ?

a) speed only

b) speed and frequency

c) speed and wavelength

d) wavelength only

e) wavelength and frequency

Question 64 - 67 use the following information

The potential difference at W is twice the potential difference at Y.

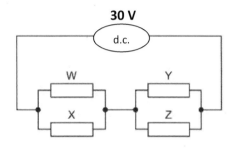

64. If a current of 5 A flows thru resistor X, what is the resistance of X ?

a)   2   Ω

b)   3   Ω

c)   3.5   Ω

d)   4   Ω

e)   5   Ω

65. If resistor Z has a resistance of 2 Ω, what is the current passing thru Z ?

a)   1   A

b)   2   A

c)   3   A

d)   4   A

e)   5   A

66. What is the power dissipated by the resistor X ?

a)   100   W

b)   75   W

c)   50   W

d)   25   W

e)   10   W

67. What is the total resistance of the circuit if the current thru W and X are equal and the current thru Y and Z are also equal ?

a)   150   Ω

b)   85   Ω

c)   50   Ω

d)   3   Ω

e)   1.5   Ω

SAT Physics Practice-Test

Question 68 - 70 use the following information

A spring with a spring constant of 4 N/cm mounted to the wall is compressed by a swinging pendulum bob of mass 100g.

68. If the spring is compressed by 5 cm then at what velocity will the pendulum move ?

a)   3.26   cm/s

b)   8.12   cm/s

c)   14.3   cm/s

d)   25.4   cm/s

e)   31.6   cm/s

69. Ignoring heat loss or friction, how high will the pendulum rise ?

a)   0.2   cm

b)   0.5   cm

c)   1.8   cm

d)   5.2   cm

e)   9.8   cm

70. If the spring is removed immediately, given that a pendulum of length 20 cm will have a period of

a)   0.2   second

b)   0.5   second

c)   0.9   second

d)   1.2   seconds

e)   1.7   seconds

71. Which of the following must be TRUE about a car that has no unbalanced force applied ?

      (I) The car does not move

      (II) The car has zero acceleration

      (III) The car has no resultant force

a)   (I) only

b)   (II) only

c)   (I) and (II) only

d)   (I) and (III) only

e)   (II) and (III) only

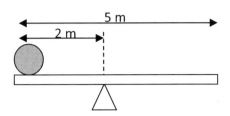

72. A uniform bar of mass 30 kg is balanced by a rock of mass M. What is the value of M ?

a)   2.5   kg

b)   5.0   kg

c)   7.5   kg

d)   9.3   kg

e)   11.5   kg

74. Radon $^{222}_{86}Ra$ decay by emitting alpha and beta to bismuth $^{214}_{83}Bi$. For this decay, how many alpha and beta particles are emitted off ?

a)   2 alpha and 1 beta

b)   2 alpha and 2 beta

c)   2 alpha and 3 beta

d)   3 alpha and 2 beta

e)   3 alpha and 3 beta

73. What is the angular velocity of a disc that spins at the rate of 300 rev per min ?

a)   0.34   rad/s

b)   3.14   rad/s

c)   31.4   rad/s

d)   34.1   rad/s

e)   341   rad/s

75. How many electrons orbits the nucleus of an isotope of hydrogen H-2 ?

a)   0

b)   1

c)   2

d)   3

e)   4

Answer Key 4

Question	Answer	Explanation
1.	D	As the ball rolls down the incline the acceleration will get smaller due to frictional force opposing it
2.	E	The graph is a projectile graph of the object falling down from the peak
3.	A	Acceleration due to gravity remains constant throughout the fall of the bottle
4.	C	Gravitational potential energy is decreasing as the height of the trooper is decreasing
5.	B	The only graph that shows a square relationship here $KE = 1/2\ m\ v^2$ $Y = k\ x^2$
6.	D	Applying law of conservation of energy here $KE = PE$ $1/2\ mv^2 = m\ g\ h$ $v^2 = 2\ (10)(15)$ $v = 17.3\ m/s$
7.	D	Not enough KE to push the ball back to the same height due to frictional loss
8.	E	$\Delta GPE = GPE_f - GPE_i$ $\Delta GPE = (5)(10)(15) - (5)(10)(-15)$ $\Delta GPE = 1500\ J$
9.	B	Area under the graphs = displacement $= 1/2 \times 5 \times 20 - 1/2 \times 3 \times 12$ $= 32\ m$
10.	D	Average speed = total distance / total time Average speed = $(50 + 18) / 8 = 8.5\ m/s$
11.	C	Slope = acceleration = $32 / 5 = 6.4\ m/s^2$
12.	A	Average velocity = total displacement / total time Average velocity = $28/15$ Average velocity = 1.86 or $1.9\ m/s$
13.	C	Ideal resistor produces no heat so the graph of current vs voltage will be a linear graph that pass thru the origin

Question	Answer	Explanation
14.	B	Thermistor's resistance varies inversely as the change in temperature occurs
15.	A	Diode works when a voltage of more than 0.7 V is applied to it
16.	D	Filament lamp will give off both heat and light as current pass thru
17.	E	LDR is known as light independent resistor whose resistance changes according to brightness of light
18.	C	We find R_{total} = 8 + 2 = 10Ω $V_T = I_T R_T$ 20 = I_T (10) I_T = 2 A Power = I^2R → connected in series so I at all point is 2 A Power = $(2)^2$ (8) = 32 watts
19.	B	As the charge passes thru electric field only vertical component of force will change ,when it is closer to the plate the field is stronger. While the horizontal component is not affected, hence it will move with constant velocity
20.	B	We apply Snell's law AIR MEDIUM A $n_1 \sin\theta_1$ = $n_2 \sin\theta_2$ 1 xsin(45) = 1.43 sinθ θ = 28.5
21.	D	We apply Snell's law AIR MEDIUM B $n_1 V_1$ = $n_2 V_2$ 1 x 3 x 10^8 = 1.43 x V V = 2.4 x 10^8 m/s
22.	A	The only choice that is true here is (I) entering and emerging angles will be equal. Medium A is more dense than medium B due to its refractive index
23.	E	None of them are true for image produced by flat mirror
24.	D	Focal point is always at the hole (lens)
25.	D	Sound wave is the only wave here that have already been polarized, all the other are electromagnetic waves which can still be polarized.

Question	Answer	Explanation
26.	B	We use $\Delta L = \alpha\, L_i\, \Delta T$ $\Delta L = 12 \times 10^{-6} \times 45 \times 50$ $\Delta L = 0.027$ cm
27.	A	Mercury is denser than aluminum We can also say that mass of mercury atoms are greater than mass of aluminum atoms in other words
28.	D	$Q = \Delta U + W$ $-3000 = -6500 + W$ $W = 3500$ Joules
29.	E	The ethanol was in liquid state at the beginning of the graph until enough heat is supplied for it to get ready to evaporates or boils
30.	C	Energy = Power x time Energy = 2.5 k x (6 x 60) Energy = 900 k J
31.	E	Heat is supply to the system by the heater through phase 1 to 3
32.	B	$Q = m\, c\, \Delta t$ $Q = 0.6 \times 4200 \times 30$ $Q = 75600$ J
33.	E	$T = 2\pi$ [square root of (L/g)] $T = 0.314$ seconds Top left to top right will be half of the period $= 0.314 / 2 = 0.157$ seconds
34.	A	$V = \omega R = 2\pi R / T$ $V = 2\pi \times 0.1 / 0.314$ $V = 2$ m/s
35.	E	$F = m v^2 / R$ $F = 0.2 \times (2)^2 / 0.1$ $F = 8$ N
36.	B	Total y component of force = 10 - 12sin30 = 10 - 6 = 4 N

Question	Answer	Explanation
37.	B

Applying Pythagoras

$R^2 = 6^2 + 6^2$
$R = 6\sqrt{2}$ m |
| 38. | B |

Clock-wise moment = Anti clock-wise moment
$\quad\quad$ 200 (1.5) $\quad$ = $\quad\quad$ F (3)
$\quad\quad\quad\quad$ F $\quad\quad$ = $\quad\quad$ 100 N |
| 39. | C | F_{net} $\quad$ = F $\quad$ - ƒ
ma $\quad$ = 120 - ƒ
4(5) = 120 - ƒ
$\quad$ ƒ $\quad$ = $\quad$ 100 $\quad$ N |
| 40. | C | Momentum of M1 $\quad$ = $\quad$ Momentum of M2
$\quad\quad\quad\quad$ M_1 (3v) $\quad$ = $\quad$ M_2 (v)
$\quad\quad\quad\quad$ M_1 / M_2 = v/3v
$\quad\quad\quad\quad$ M_1 / M_2 = 1/3 |

Question	Answer	Explanation
41.	A	$a = \dfrac{GM_{planet}}{R^2}$ $\dfrac{a_{planet}}{a_{Earth}} = \dfrac{GM_{planet}}{R^2_{planet}} \div \dfrac{GM_{Earth}}{R^2_{Earth}}$ $= \dfrac{GM_{planet}}{R^2_{planet}} \times \dfrac{R^2_{Earth}}{GM_{Earth}}$ $= \dfrac{G\ M}{4R^2} \times \dfrac{R^2}{GM}$ $= 1/4$
42.	C	$u = 0$ m/s, $a = 3$ m/s^2 , $t = 6$ s, $s = ??$ $s = ut + 1/2\ a\ t^2$ $s = 0\,(6) + 1/2\,(3)\,(6^2)$ $s = 54$ m
43.	B	$\Delta p = m\,\Delta v = 5000\,(0 - 25) = 125000$ N·s $\Delta p = 125$ kN·s
44.	D	Power = force x velocity Power = force x distance / time Power = energy / time
45.	B	Weight / area = force / area = Pressure
46.	A	Alpha has a greatest ionizing effect than all type of radaition
47.	E	Radioactive isotopes have some number of proton/s but different number of neutron/s
48.	E	0 day → 20 days → 40 days → 60 days → 80 days → 100 days 320 g 160 g 80 g 40 g 20 g <u>10 g</u>
49.	D	Neutron is heavisest of all listed and also located at the center
50.	E	A bundle of photons oscillating freely are in form of electromagnetic waves
51.	B	Positron have similar mass to electron but opposite charge (positively charged)
52.	C	Electrons are eemitted during beta decay
53.	B	T^2 is directly proportional to length L of a pendulum

Question	Answer	Explanation
54.	A	$a_g = Gm/r^2$ acceleration due to gravity varies inversely as radius of the planet square
55.	E	$F_g = Gm_1m_2 / r^2$ Gravitational force between planets varies directly as the product of the planet's masses
56.	D	$V_{orbit} = \sqrt{\dfrac{GM}{R}}$ Orbital velocity varies inversely as the square root of the planet's radius
57.	C	$\Delta L = m\,v\,r$ Angular momentum varies as the product of mass and radius
58.	B	A diode has an operating voltage of 0.7 V
59.	D	Pitch of a wave is affected directly by the frequency of the wave
60.	B	$E = V/D$ $V_1/D_1 = V_2/D_2$ $6/10 = V/5$ $V_2 = 3$ volt Change in electric potential $= V_2 - V_1 = 3 - 6 = -3$ V
61.	D	$U = q\,V$ $U = 2 \times 6$ $U = 12$ Joules
62.	C	Electron will be attracted towards the positive plate, hence it will curved up
63.	C	Monochromatic light will always be moving with the same frequency towards any medium
64.	D	We know that $V_w + V_y = V_{total}$ $\qquad\qquad 2V_y + V_y = 30$ $\qquad\qquad\qquad V_y = 10$ Volt $V_x = V_w = 2V_y = 20$ volt $V_x = I_x R_x$ $20 = (5)(R_x)$ $R_x = 4\ \Omega$

Question	Answer	Explanation
65.	E	We know that $V_z = V_y = 10$ Volt $I_z R_z = 10$ $I_z (2) = 10$ $I_z = 5A$
66.	A	$P_x = I_x V_x$ $P_x = 5 \times 20 = 100$ W
67.	D	$I_{total} = I_w + I_x = 5 + 5 = 10$ A $V_{total} = I_{total} \times R_{total}$ $30 = (10) R_{total}$ $R_{total} = 3\ \Omega$
68.	E	$EPE = KE$ $1/2\ k\ x^2 = 1/2\ m\ v^2$ $(4)(5)^2 = (0.1)\ v^2$ $v = 31.6$ cm/s
69.	B	$GPE = KE$ $mgh = 1/2\ m\ v^2$ $(10)(h) = 1/2\ (0.316)^2$ $h = 0.00499$ m or 0.5 cm
70.	C	$T = 2\pi \sqrt{\dfrac{L}{g}} = 2\pi \sqrt{\dfrac{0.2}{10}} = 0.9$ s
71.	E	No unbalanced force = balanced force Which means the car could be moving or at rest but we know for sure that there will be no acceleration and no resultant force
72.	C	Total anti-clockwise moment = Total clockwise moment $Mg (2) = (300)(0.5)$ $M = 7.5$ kg
73.	B	$\omega = 2\pi f = 2\pi (300/60) = 31.4$ rad/s
74.	A	$^{222}_{86}Ra \rightarrow 2\,^{4}_{2}He + ^{0}_{-1}e + ^{214}_{83}Bi$ From here we have 2 alpha (in form of helium atoms) and 1 beta (in form of an electron)
75.	B	Hydrogen isotopes of H-2 has 1 proton, 1 neutron and 1 electron only

Score Range

Raw Score	Conversion
65 - 75	800
59 - 64	750 - 790
53 - 58	720 - 740
48 - 52	690 - 710
42 - 47	650 - 680
36 - 41	590 - 640
30 - 35	540 - 580
25 - 29	510 - 530
20 - 24	450 - 500
15 - 19	400 - 440
0 - 15	270 - 390

Raw Score = Correct Answers - 0.25 Wrong Answers

$$\boxed{} = \boxed{} - 0.25 \times \boxed{}$$

Key words

A

Absorber - A substance that takes in radiation

Alpha Radiation - Alpha particles, Each consists of 2 Protons and 2 Neutrons (A Helium Nucleus),emitted by unstable nuclei

Alternating Current - Electric current in a circuit that repeatedly changes direction

Amplitude - The height of a wave crest from trough to the rest position, maximum Distance moved by an object from its equilibrium position

Angle of Incidence - Angle between the incident ray and the normal

Angle of Reflection - Angle between the reflected ray and the normal

Atomic Number - The number of protons in an atom

B

Beta Radiation - High energy electrons that are created in and emitted from unstable nuclei

Biofuel - Fuel made from animal and plant products

Black Hole - An object in space that has so much mass, that nothing, not even light, can escape from its gravitational field

C

Centre of Mass - The point where an object's mass may be thought to be concentrated

Centripetal Acceleration - The acceleration of an object moving in a circle at a constant speed. Centripetal acceleration always acts towards the centre of the circle

Centripetal Force - The resultant force towards the centre of a circle acting on an object moving in a circular path

Chain Reaction - Reactions in which one reaction causes further reactions, which in turn cause further reactions

Chain Reaction of Nuclear Fission - When fission neutrons cause further fission, so more fission neutrons are released. This goes on to produce further fission

Chemical Potential Energy - Energy stored in form of chemical

Circuit Breaker - An electromagnetic switch that opens and cuts the current off if too much current passes through it

Compression - high pressure of particles

Condensation - Turning from a vapour into a liquid

Conduction - Transfer of energy from particle to particle in matter via free electrons

Conductor - Material or Object that conducts heat or electricity

Conservation Of Energy - Energy cannot be created or destroyed (It can only be transferred)
Conservation Of Momentum - In a closed system, the momentum before an event is equal to the total momentum after the event. Momentum is conserved in any collision or explosion provided that no external forces act on the objects that collide or explode.
Convection - Transfer of energy in fluid
Convection Current - The circular motion of matter caused by the heating in fluids
Converging Lens - A lens that makes light rays parallel to the principal axis converge to a point
Convex Lens - Converging Lens
Concave Lens - Diverging Lens
Critical Angle -The angle of incidence of a light ray in a transparent substance which produces refraction
Crumple Zone - Region of a vehicle designed to crumple in a collision to reduce the force on the occupants

D

Diffraction - The spreading of waves when they pass through a gap or around the edges of an obstacle that has a similar size as the wavelength of the waves
Diode - Electrical device that allows current flow in one direction only
Doppler Effect - The change of wavelength (and frequency) of the waves from a moving source due to the motion of the source towards or away from the observer
Drag Force - A force opposing the motion of an object due to fluid (e.g air) flowing past the object as it moves

E

Echo - Reflection of sound that can be heard
Efficiency - Useful Energy transferred by a device ÷ total energy supplied to the device
Effort - The force applied to a device used to raise a weight or shift an object
Elastic - A material is elastic if it is able to regain its shape after it has be squashed or stretched
Elastic Potential Energy - Energy stored in an elastic object when work is done to change its shape
Electrical Energy - Energy transferred by the movement of electrical charge
Electromagnetic Induction - The process of introducing a potential difference in a wire by moving the wire so it cuts along the lines of force of a magnetic field
Electromagnetic Wave - Electric and magnetic disturbance that transfers energy from one place to another
Electron - A tiny particle with a negative charge Electrons orbit the nucleus in atoms or ions.
Emitter - A substance that gives out radiation
Equilibrium - The state of an object when it is at rest
Evaporation - Turning from a liquid to vapour

F

Fluid - A liquid or a gas

Focal Length - The distance from the centre of a lens to the point where light rays parallel to the principal axis are focused

Fossil Fuel - Fuel obtained from long dead biological material

Frequency - The number of wave crests passing a fixed point every second (measures in Hertz)

Friction - Forces opposing the movement of one surface over another

Fuse - Contains a thin wire that melts and cuts the current if too much current is passing through it

G

Gamma Radiation - Electromagnetic Radiation emitted from unstable nuclei in radioactive substances

Gamma Ray - The highest energy eaves in the electromagnetic spectrum

Generator - A machine generates electricity by conversion of energy

Geothermal Energy - Energy from hot underground rocks

Gravitational Attraction - Force that pulls two masses together

H

Half-Life - Average time taken for the number of nuclei of the isotope (or mass of the isotope) in a sample to halve

Hooke's Law - The extension of a spring is directly proportional to the force applied provided the limit is not exceeded

Hydraulic Pressure - The pressure in a liquid in a hydraulic arm

I

Infrared Radiation - Electromagnetic waves between visible light and microwaves in the electromagnetic spectrum

Input Energy - Energy supplied to a machine

Insulating - Reducing energy transfer by heating

Insulator - Material or object that is a poor conductor of heat and electrons

Ion - A charged particle that is produced by the loss or gain of electrons

Ionisation - Any process in which atoms become charged

Isotope - Atom that has the same number of protons but a different number of neutrons. It has the same atomic number but a different mass number

L

LDR (Light Dependent Resistor) - Device with a resistance that varies with the amount of light falling on it

Limit of Proportionality - The limit for Hooke's Law applied to the extension of a stretched spring.

Load - The weight of an object raised by the a device used to lift the object or the force applied by a device to shift an object

Longitudinal Wave - Wave in which the vibrations are parallel to the direction of energy transfer.

M

Machine - A device in which a force applied at a point produces another force at another point

Magnifying Glass - A converging lens used to magnify a small object that must be placed between the lens and the focal point

Mass Number - The total number of protons and neutrons in an atom

Mechanical Wave - Wave that travels through a substance

Microwave - Part of the electromagnetic spectrum

N

National Grid - The network of cables and transformers used to transfer electricity from power stations to consumers

Neutral Wire - The wire of a main circuit that is earthed at the local substation so its potential is close to zero

Neutron - A no charge particle found in the nucleus

Non-renewable - Something that cannot be replaced once it is used up

Normal - Straight line through a surface or boundary perpendicular to it

Nucleus - The very small and dense central part of an atom composed of proton and neutron

O

Ohm's Law - The current through a resistor is directly proportional to the potential difference across a resistor

Ohmic Conductor - A conductor that has a constant resistance and therefore obeys Ohm's law

Optical Fiber - Thin glass fiber used to send light signals along

Oscillation - movement of wave in particular direction

P

Parallel - Components connected in a circuit so that the potential difference is the same across each one

Pitch - The frequency of a sound wave

Potential Difference - A measure of the work done or energy transferred per coulomb of charge.

Power - The amount energy transferred per second

Pressure - Force per unit area for a force acting on a surface at right angles to the surface

Principal Axis - A straight line that passes along the normal at the centre of each lens surface

Principal Focus - The point where light rays parallel to the principal axis are focused

Proton - A positively charged particle found inside the nucleus of an atom

R

Radio wave - Longest wavelength of the electromagnetic spectrum

Real Image - An image that forms where light rays meet and can be projected on the screen

Reflector - A surface that reflects radiation

Refraction - The change of direction of a light ray when it passes across a boundary between two transparent substances

Renewable Energy - Energy from sources that never run out

Resistance - Anything that slows the flow of current in a circuit, measures in Ohms

Resultant Force - The combined effect of the forces acting on an object

S

Series - Components connected in a circuit so that the same current that passes through them are in series with each other

Solar Cell - Electrical Cell that produces a voltage when in sunlight. Usually connected together in solar cell panels

Solar Energy - Energy from the sun

Sound - A form of mechanical energy

Specific Heat Capacity - Energy needed by 1kg to raise its temperature by 1°c

Step-Down Transformer - Electrical Device that is used to step down the size of an alternating voltage

Step-Up Transformer - Electrical Device that is used to step up the size of an alternating voltage

T

Temperature - The degree of hotness or coldness of a substance

Terminal Velocity - The velocity reached by an object when the drag force on it is equal and opposite to the force making it move

Thermistor - Device with a resistance that varies with temperature

Total Internal Reflection - When the angle of incidence of a light ray in a transparent substance is greater than the critical angle. This means that the angle of reflection is equal to the angle of incidence

Transformer - Electrical device used to change a voltage

Transverse Waves - Waves in which the vibrations are perpendicular to the direction of energy transfer

U

Ultrasound Wave - Sound wave at a frequency greater than 20 000 Hz

Ultraviolet Radiation - Electromagnetic radiation just beyond the blue end of the visible spectrum

V

Virtual Image - An image seen in a lens or a mirror from which light rays appear to come after being refracted by the lens or reflected on a mirror. It cannot be projected

W

Wasted Energy - Energy that is not usefully transferred

Wave - a method of transferring energy

Wavelength - The distance from one wave crest to the next wave crest (along the waves)

Work - amount of energy transferred or changed

X

X-Ray - High energy wave from the part of the electromagnetic spectrum between gamma and ultraviolet waves

Appendix I

Units Conversion

Prefixes	Value	Standard form	Symbol
Tera	1,000,000,000,000	10^{12}	T
Giga	1,000,000,000	10^{9}	G
Mega	1,000,000	10^{6}	M
Kilo	1,000	10^{3}	k
deci	0.1	10^{-1}	d
centi	0.01	10^{-2}	c
milli	0.001	10^{-3}	m
micro	0.000001	10^{-6}	μ
nano	0.000000001	10^{-9}	n
pico	0.000000000001	10^{-12}	p

Rules for trigonometry

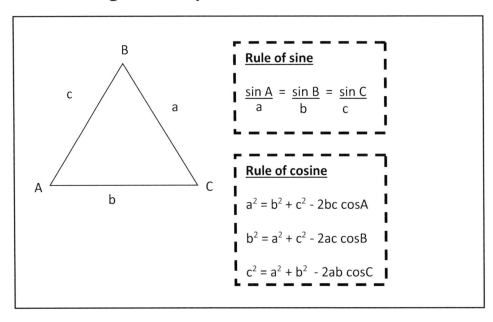

Rule of sine

$$\frac{\sin A}{a} = \frac{\sin B}{b} = \frac{\sin C}{c}$$

Rule of cosine

$$a^2 = b^2 + c^2 - 2bc \cos A$$

$$b^2 = a^2 + c^2 - 2ac \cos B$$

$$c^2 = a^2 + b^2 - 2ab \cos C$$

Appendix II

Mechanics

speed $= \dfrac{\text{change in distance}}{\text{change in time}}$

velocity $= \dfrac{\text{change in displacement}}{\text{change in time}}$

Average speed $= \dfrac{\text{total distance}}{\text{total time}}$

Average velocity $= \dfrac{\text{total displacement}}{\text{total time}}$

Acceleration $= \dfrac{\text{change in velocity}}{\text{change in time}}$

Equation of motion

	Missing term
$v = u + at$	s
$s = ut + 1/2\, at^2$	v
$v^2 = u^2 + 2as$	t
$s = \dfrac{(u + v)\, t}{2}$	a

circular motion

$s = \theta R$

$v = \omega R$

$\omega = 2\pi f$

$a = \alpha R$

Forces

$F = m a$

$f = \mu N$

$W = m g$

$F = k X$

$F_c = m a_c$

$a_c = \dfrac{v^2}{R}$

Energy

Work $=$ force x distance

$KE = \dfrac{1}{2} m\, v^2$

$GPE = m g h$

$EPE = \dfrac{1}{2} k\, X^2$

Power $= \dfrac{\text{Work}}{\Delta \text{time}} = \dfrac{\Delta \text{energy}}{\Delta \text{time}}$

Momentum

$p = m \cdot v$

$\Delta p = m \cdot \Delta v$

$\Delta p = F \cdot \Delta t$

Torque

$\dagger = F \cdot d$

In equilibrium

$\Sigma \dagger_{acw} = \Sigma \dagger_{cw}$

$\Delta L = m \times \Delta v \times r$

Thermal Properties

Pressure

$P = \dfrac{F}{A}$

$P = h \, \rho \, g$

$PV = n R T$

Thermal expansion

$\Delta L = \alpha \, L_i \, \Delta T$

$\Delta V = \beta \, V_i \, \Delta T$

Heat energy

$Q = m \times c \times \Delta T$

$Q_f = m \times H_f$

$Q_v = m \times H_v$

$Q = \Delta U + W$

Waves

$v = f \cdot \lambda$

$f = \dfrac{1}{T}$

$v = \sqrt{\dfrac{T}{\mu}}$

Beats = |Frequency$_1$ - Frequency$_2$ |

angle of incidence = angle of reflection

Snell's Law

$n_1 \sin(\theta_1) = n_2 \sin(\theta_2)$

$n = \dfrac{1}{\sin \theta_c}$

Intensity $= \dfrac{1}{distance^2}$

Double slit

$\dfrac{\lambda}{D} = \dfrac{X}{L}$

Mirror and Lens

$M = \dfrac{d_i}{d_o} = \dfrac{h_i}{h_o}$

$\dfrac{1}{f} = \dfrac{1}{d_i} + \dfrac{1}{d_o}$

$\dfrac{1}{f} = \dfrac{1}{h_i} + \dfrac{1}{h_o}$

SHM

$T = 2\pi \sqrt{\dfrac{L}{g}}$

$T = 2\pi \sqrt{\dfrac{m}{k}}$

Field and Potentials

Gravitaional field

$$K_s = \frac{R^3}{T^2}$$

$$F_g = \frac{G\,m_1\,m_2}{R^2}$$

$$a_g = \frac{G\,m}{R^2}$$

$$\Delta U = -\frac{G\,m_{object} \cdot m_{Earth}}{R}$$

$$V_{escape} = \sqrt{\frac{2GMe}{Re}}$$

$$V_{orbit} = \sqrt{\frac{GMe}{Re}}$$

Electric field

$$F_e = \frac{K\,q_1\,q_2}{R^2}$$

$$E = \frac{kq}{R^2}$$

$$V = E \ D$$

$$U = q \ V$$

Electricity

$$V = I \cdot R$$

$$P = I \cdot V$$

$$I = \frac{\Delta Q}{\Delta t}$$

$$\varepsilon = I\,R + I\,r$$

$$R = \frac{\rho\,L}{A}$$

$$Q = C\,V$$

$$U = \frac{Q\,V}{2}$$

Magnetism

$$B = \frac{\mu_0\,I}{2\pi R}$$

$$F = B\,I\,L$$

$$F = q\,v\,B$$

$$\Phi = B \cdot A$$

Electromagnetic induction

$$P_{input} = P_{output}$$

$$V_{input} \times I_{input} = V_{output} \times I_{output}$$

Quantum

$E = hf$

$E_K = hf - \Phi$

$p = \dfrac{h}{\lambda}$

$E = m c^2$

$A_n = \dfrac{A_0}{2^n}$

$M_n = \dfrac{M_0}{2^n}$

$T = t_0 \cdot \Upsilon = \dfrac{t_0}{\sqrt{1 - (v/c)^2}}$

$L = L_0 \div \Upsilon = L_0 \cdot \sqrt{1 - (v/c)^2}$

$m = m_0 \cdot \Upsilon = \dfrac{m_0}{\sqrt{1 - (v/c)^2}}$

Appendix III

Fundamental Constant

Quantity	Symbol	Value
Acceleration due to gravity	g	$9.81 \text{ m/s}^2 \approx 10 \text{ m/s}^2$
Gravitational constant	G	$6.67 \times 10^{-11} \text{ Nm}^2 / \text{kg}^2$
Gas constant	R	$8.31 \text{ J K}^{-1} \text{ mol}^{-1}$
Coulomb constant	k	$9 \times 10^{9} \text{ N m}^2 \text{ C}^{-2}$
Permeability of free space	μ_0	$4\pi \times 10^{-7} \text{ T m A}^{-1}$
Planck's constant	h	$6.63 \times 10^{-34} \text{ J s}$
Speed of light (in Air and Vacuum)	c	$3 \times 10^8 \text{ m/s}$
Charge on Proton and electron	e	$1.6 \times 10^{-19} \text{ C}$
Mass of electron	m_e	$9.11 \times 10^{-31} \text{ kg}$
Mass of proton	m_p	$1.673 \times 10^{-27} \text{ kg}$
Mass of neutron	M_n	$1.675 \times 10^{-27} \text{ kg}$
Electron-Volt	$1eV$	$1.6 \times 10^{-19} \text{ J}$

SAT Physics Practice-Test

Made in the USA
San Bernardino, CA
21 April 2017